The Compact Book of
FISH & GAME COOKERY

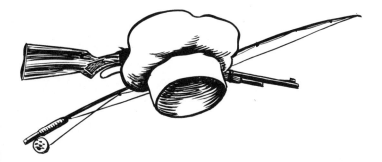

The Compact Book of
FISH & GAME COOKERY

by Lawton Carver

Illustrated by Francis W. Davis

GRAMERCY PUBLISHING COMPANY • NEW YORK

INTRODUCTION

Cooking has been a part of literary effort and controversy for approximately 2,500 years and as early as 1475 a few kitchen shelves included De Honesta Voluptate, the first cook book put into type. Since then they have been produced in a growing flood of recipe-laden pages.

It is likely that through these centuries more books have been written on cookery than any other technical subject except love. The latter, however, most often is presented as fictionalized romance, leaving little or no room for dispute.

Cook books are instructive on a form of creativity similar to painting, composing music or cutting a rug with the Watusi. Because everybody has his own preference in the food he eats, the pictures he looks at, the music he listens to and proper epileptic presentation of the dance, some among any collection of recipes must conflict with individual tastes.

Therefore, let it be said and known that this book was put together to make available to others our experiences through a number of years in preparing fish and game and watching many practitioners at it. If you've got any arguments save them for the shades of Careme, Escoffier and the other all-time great all-around maitres de cuisine.

The preparations in this book are the survivors of scores of them we have encountered while running restaurants and loafing in shooting and fishing lodges and camps. Many other recipes have been discarded for one reason or another. These herein will be found practical for the most part with use of stove and some contents of a nearby grocery, not overlooking frozen foods when the very fresh are not available.

Finally all this will work in the open, too, although not recommended. Outdoor camp chefs have been known to lose weight and become perilously weak from the constant exercise of fighting ants and other insects. Outdoor cookery indoors is better.

LAWTON CARVER

CONTENTS

CHAPTER 1

In an Emergency, It's All Good to Eat if it Doesn't Bite Back

The one out of every five Americans who hunts or fishes —or both—usually regards himself as a superior cook, indoors or out, and it is a fact that nearly everybody who spends time in the woods for whatever reason can fix up a meal of sorts. Among them, there are a few who do a superlatively fine job of it. These are the ones who know the difference between good and mediocre—or plain bad— whether they are eating beneath leafy boughs or a crystal chandelier.

To the less able outdoor chef de cuisine, the suggestion is herewith offered that it is a fallacy to suppose that, through secrets known only to woodsmen, food unpalatable to taste or to contemplate can be made appealing to more civilized appetites. Such food can be improved when properly disguised, but rarely does it become a worthwhile delicacy fit for any occasion other than an emergency. The insistence here is that fishducks, porcupines, muskrats and the like are good only to prevent starvation when you are lost, injured, snowblind, caught between the rocks, or drunk.

In these aforementioned exigencies it is recommended that, without regard for taste or appearance of a likely meal, you eat anything that won't bite back. Even a man's old rawhide boot-laces have been described as quite tasty under proper

9

stress, but to suggest that they would be acceptable as part of a properly prepared meal would be as valid as saying that anybody who can take game and fish is a taxidermist.

There is enough good outdoor food so that you will find no tricks in this book for making bad food good, not even a hint—if there is one—as to how polar bear liver can be prepared so that its reputed overload of vitamins won't kill you.

In game and fish cookery there is a right and a wrong which are as basic as the approach to wing-shooting, fly-casting or any other endeavour involving the outdoors. There is no obscure sorcery involved. Being able to build a camp-fire which doesn't spread half way across the continent and yet will provide ample heat for cooking is essential, if you are cooking outdoors, but the actual starting point, outdoors or indoors, is to know whether the food is fresh or stale, young or old. There is a difference between staleness and properly aged and in the case of fish in particular staleness well may be spelled ptomaine.

Old game will require long moist cooking and even then it often will be barely fit to eat. Equally bad is overcooking young game, especially several kinds that come under the heading of venison. Overcooking dries out and tends to toughen meat as naturally dry and fat-free as is most game.

As for aging, a point of occasional dispute, proper storing for the proper length of time will enhance the flavor of meat and do some tenderizing. Feathered game and small game will be better for having hung 3 or 5 days at a temperature 6 or 7 degrees above freezing, if such refrigeration is available. In the woods this will be governed by conditions, but it can be pointed out that game spoils quickly in warm weather and does not age if frozen. Young venison will be better after aging a week and old venison can stand two weeks. By venison is meant all the antlered game—deer, moose, caribou and elk.

Of the big game, bear meat is the least desirable with the majority. It is fatty, stringy and flavored by an omnivorous diet that ranges from fruit and nuts, to available meat and grubs and including carrion. Even young bear is rich, somewhat like pork, and like pork, may be infected with trichinosis, requiring long cooking. Too much bear can be sickening, whereas other game may be eaten without ill effects until you start to grunt with fullness. Then do like the Mountain Men of old. Take a nap, and eat some more.

They were lucky in the amount of game and the variety at hand. Today, game too often is tough with age or of a poor type, in which case forget about trying to fix it up so it is fit to eat simply because it is game and regarded as a rare treat. With a grandiose gesture, give this kind to somebody you hate.

What this book purports to do is bring to you recipes for so-called outdoor dishes the way they are served in better restaurants, in camps and lodges and by woodsmen who through good taste and long practice qualify as good cooks.

Roasting and broiling have been the favorite methods of cooking going back farther than anybody can remember—like a million years, when perhaps a flash of lightning struck dead one of our ancestors and his hungry friends discovered that he tasted much better thus seared rather than plumb raw.

This led eventually to the larding needle, the meat thermometer, heat-controlled ovens, backyard Bar-B-Ques, cook books and to gourmets whose palates can be titillated only if their wild meat has been hung and aged to the point of incipient putrifaction.

This cult also insists that the only way to roast a bird is with its head· on and neatly tucked under a wing for esthetic appeal, its feet on for the same reason, the intestines left in and the vent not removed. An incision, they say, would impair the flavor. We will continue to risk that, rather than eat a bird not thoroughly cleaned, despite what history tells us of other days and what we know of current practices in the use of un-drawn game.

We know, for instance, that all the way back to the Bacchanalian days of the Roman Empire they pounded intestines of one kind or another into their more precious sauces, and this custom still prevails. Escoffier, probably the greatest of chefs, adheres to that notion and in his recipes for woodcock, for instance, he specifies that the bird's intestines should be minced and added to some dishes, including woodcock Favart, salmis of woodcock and Woodcock Careme, the latter named for perhaps the all-time second best chef.

You'll find none of Escoffier's such strange recipes in this book and none of his details for proper preparation of friendly little song birds, such as thrushes, larks, black birds and warblers. They are better off singing.

Not that you have to be a Frenchman to eat little birds. The Italians knock off sparrows by the bushel with nets and, as regards intestines as a delicacy, stuffed and broiled, they are finest of holiday fare for Southern Italians, whose taste in this department runs mainly to young goats. The English call cooked venison entrails umbles. In our own South, intestines, generally from hogs and cooked with seasonings and spices and greens, are known as chitterlings.

Tripe, the stomach of a ruminating animal, is famous the world over as prepared by the French through some eight hours of slow cooking and celebrated also when creamed with onions and oysters, or boiled, breaded and fried, among numerous other preparations. The Scotch stuff a sheep's stomach with oatmeal mash that includes chopped animal innards and boil it forever. Finally, to the skirl of pipers, they stick a sword in it and, as the steam and liquid geyser, keep on drinking while the guest of honor recites to the pudding from Bobby Burns:

"Fair fa' you honest sonsie face,
Great chieftain o' the puddin' race!
Aboon them a' ye tak' your place,
Painch, tripe or thairm;
Weel are ye worthy o' a grace—
As lang's my arm."

You don't have to be drunk on Scotch, but it helps, to enjoy this oddball example of foodstuff known to the perpetrators as Haggis, one of the oldest of ceremonial table offerings wherever hardy, outdoor type killer-dillers gather.

Then, too, there is the liver, also the lung, gizzard, kidney

and the gland called sweetbreads, all of which are rich in vitamins, we are told, and pigs' and calves' feet contain gelatin as does hartshorn, the shavings from deer antlers. Oxtail soup is a staple and the tails and jowls of hogs are mighty tasty, so they say, done up just right. Tongue? From the bison it attracted the notice of monarchs of another day. From lesser, more abundant animals it is a supermarket special. Venison 'brains are highly recommended as camp fare —plain pan-fried, scrambled with eggs or fried into fritters.

In the other direction of the carcass, cowboys not only enjoy the subtle flavor of mountain oysters—the testicles of calves removed to convert bulls into steers—but are comforted by the belief that this alleged rare treat, which comes neither from the mountains nor the sea, increases a fellow's bedroom virility. Mountain oysters are most prized at round-up time, simply roasted in the live coals and ash of the branding fire, or sometimes made into a savory ranch breakfast with hot biscuits and molasses.

Thus we find that almost all parts of birds and animals are edible, from stem to stern and through the beam, from keel to as high as there is anything to carve and to be eaten with appreciative grunts—no matter how repelling some of the viands may be to rank and file gourmets. In fairness, it can be said that those with strange eating habits may have a point that escapes more plebeian taste. Anyway, if they like their game hung until the smell is enough to evacuate a community, then cooked without inside cleaning at all, they can't be arrested for it but should be. This all comes under the heading of personal choice, let's say, as the old lady remarked kissing a goat.

However, most outdoorsmen—in fact, all that I have ever known—want their game aged about like beef, which is to a point somewhat short of odor, and they want it thoroughly cleaned and rinsed before cooking.

CHAPTER 2

SMALL GAME
Rabbit, Hare and Squirrel

It is estimated that Americans kill and consume approximately 50,000,000 rabbits and hares each year, putting these skittish inhabitants of fields and thickets from coast to coast at the top of the list of game bagged by hunters. The cottontail rabbit (prevalent in several species in this country,) is by far the most popular and the jack rabbit and snowshoe rabbit, both hares, the least sought after.

A young cottontail is light-meated, tasty and tender, and even older rabbits can be made edible by properly long, moist cooking. The wild hares are not of much worth, except when very young. The older ones are composed mostly of steel thews and are best dressed with a hacksaw, if at all. Whereas a rabbit will weigh up to around three pounds, a hare gets big enough to kick a hole in you at 12 pounds or so.

As small game food, squirrels would be as popular as rabbits if they were as easy to come by. To obtain a mess of rabbit requires little more than a walk in the fields in many places, kicking brush heaps and watching for a flash of white, while the hound runs off in all directions, scenting and sometimes trailing. You may walk a hickory grove all day and sit quietly at intervals, too, and get few shots, but to the squirrel-hunter it is worth the effort. Three or four grey squirrels make a pretty good mess for frying, for a Brunswick stew and for other dishes.

The grey squirrel is by far the most numerous, and young ones of a little less than a pound are delicate in flavor and tender. Fox squirrels, averaging close to two pounds, are equally good eating, but are getting scarcer all the time.

Most of the recipes in this chapter may be used interchangeably for rabbit and squirrel, both of which have a wild rather than a gamey taste, but with a slight edge in flavor going to the squirrel because of a diet composed mostly of nuts. Rabbit can be pretty dry and is low in nutrition, and by rabbit we mean also hares, including the domesticated Belgians and other such.

Nevertheless it has an international renown denied most game due to one dish in particular which is prepared much the same everywhere under different names:

German Hasen Pfeffer, French Civet de Lievre, British Jugged Hare, Southern Italian Coniglio Agrodolce, Belgian Konijnmet Pruinen, Dutch Hazenpeper, American marinated rabbit.

The approach in each is the same, with the inevitable variations to be found in all recipes, even national dishes within a given country. The Escoffiers can give you a half dozen or more recipes for the same dish as can the Howard Johnsons, covering the argument with a sign saying "Ice Cream—28 Flavors." That fits the rabbit and hare, too, there being almost no limit to what you can do once in the kitchen with same.

There was and may still be a place in Milwaukee which prepared rabbit after the fashion of Sauerbraten—with a sauce of marinade and crumbled ginger snaps. Sour cream in rabbit sauce is not uncommon. There is still another sauce which surprisingly has failed to achieve status in the United States. In this one you use juniper berries, which impart to gin and the martini a taste so delightful as to be irresistible in backyard cookouts as well as saloons.

To our way of thinking one of the best of all rabbit dishes is prepared as often as possible by some of us who gather in the New York Catskills. This is:

AMERICAN JUGGED HARE

1 rabbit or snowshoe	1 cup canned chicken broth
2 medium onions sliced	1 bay leaf
2 cups dry red wine	a dozen small white onions
½ stick butter	1 cup small cubed potatoes
½ cup small cubed bacon	1 cup button mushrooms
4 tablespoons flour	freshly ground pepper, salt

Cut rabbit into eight pieces—hindlegs, forelegs, split back and across back pieces—and place in bowl with sliced onion, and wine to marinate all day, turning occasionally. Wipe rabbit dry, saute in butter and drippings from which bacon has been removed to be returned later. When rabbit is browned add flour to brown. Add cup of marinade, and all other ingredients and simmer until done. Depending upon size of rabbit or hare, serves 2 to 4 with biscuits.

HASEN PFEFFER

Follow foregoing recipe, but use 1½ cups wine vinegar and ½ cup water, instead of wine for marinade; use butter and cooking oil instead of bacon and omit mushrooms and potatoes. Serve with potatoes, wild rice, or white rice and biscuits.

FRIED RABBIT

The late Jack Randolph, an outdoor writer of charm and warmth, was as direct in his preparation of game as he was in everything else. His version of fried rabbit—preferably the ones around the farm at Colrain, Mass.—was simply this: Salt and pepper and flour the cut up rabbit. Brown well in vegetable oil, add 4 tablespoons of water—no more—cover it, turn it once and in three or four more minutes eat it. Jack advocated and practiced soaking the cut up rabbit overnight in water to cover with about three tablespoons of salt to improve flavor. Came time to cook, he rinsed it off, wiped it dry, and fried it up.

FRIED RABBIT GRAVY

After frying rabbit, add a tablespoon of chopped chives or scallions to the skillet and saute 2 minutes. Stir in 4 tablespoons of flour, adding butter if needed. Add one cup milk and one of broth, beef or chicken, or water, and a tablespoon chopped parsley, salt and pepper. Simmer until thickened. Serve 2 or more with wild or white rice, or boiled potatoes, with guava, grape or currant jelly on the side. And hot biscuits.

A variation of the above is:

SAWMILL GRAVY

Follow the foregoing recipe and add to it ¼ teaspoon powdered mustard, 2 tablespoons catsup and a dash of Tabasco.

BARBECUED RABBIT

1 rabbit	½ cup catsup
olive oil	¼ cup water
¼ stick butter	1 teaspoon chili powder
2 buds garlic chopped	1 tablespoon lemon juice
1 small onion chopped	½ teaspoon oregano
¼ cup Worcestershire	dash Tabasco

Instead of cutting in pieces, split rabbit, rub generously with olive oil and broil over charcoal until nearly done, turning often. Meanwhile, saute garlic and onions in butter 2 minutes, add other ingredients, simmer 10 minutes, strain, brush sauce on rabbit until used up, turning often. Serves 2 or more with French fried potatoes.

BROILED RABBIT

Place young rabbit split in half over charcoal to broil, basting at start and several times thereafter with mixture of ¼ cup olive oil, ¼ cup white wine and 1 teaspoon lemon juice and add salt and pepper when rabbit is browned and done. Serves 2 or more with small, new parslied potatoes, field peas and tart grape jelly.

ROAST RABBIT JUNIPER

Before roasting, broiling or frying, some do and some don't soak the split or cut up rabbit from a few hours to overnight in a marinade or in water with about 2 teaspoons of salt to the cup. Tender young rabbits don't really need it.

1 rabbit	½ cup white wine
butter	½ cup broth or water
1 teaspoon minced onion	scant teaspoon juniper berries
1 bay leaf	salt
few drops lemon juice	freshly ground pepper

Split rabbit, smear with plenty of butter, put in roasting pan—cavity side up—and into oven pre-heated to 450. In 15 minutes add a little water to pan to prevent burning juices and lower oven to 350. Roast about 45 minutes, turning once. Remove rabbit from pan to hot plate and keep warm. Add ¼ stick of butter to pan, tablespoon flour, stir to brown lightly and add all other ingredients, juniper berries having been crushed. Strain sauce over rabbit. Serves 2 or more with parslied potatoes or baked potatoes with sour cream and chives.

RABBIT CREOLE

1 rabbit	1 green pepper in strips
¼ cup olive oil	1 bay leaf
six scallions and tops chopped	1 tablespoon chopped parsley
1 clove garlic chopped	Tabasco to taste
small can tomatoes	salt
2 cups water	4 tablespoons butter
1 stalk celery and	
leaves chopped	

Saute rabbit in olive oil until brown. Add garlic and scallions. Add all other ingredients, except butter and flour, which should be made into brown roux then added. Serves 4 with rice.

RABBIT STEW WITH DUMPLINGS

1 rabbit	water to cover
flour to dredge and	salt and pepper
2 tablespoons flour	pinch of thyme
½ stick butter	1 bay leaf
4 medium scallions and tops	1 tablespoon chopped parsley
chopped	dumplings with
1 inside stalk celery and	pinch of sage
leaves chopped	

Dredge rabbit cut in six pieces in flour, saute in butter and the 2 tablespoons of flour to brown. Add white part of scallions and reserve chopped green tops. Stir 2 minutes and add all other ingredients, except onion tops and dumplings. When the rabbit is nearly done spoon in four or five drop dumplings (see recipe in chapter on breads, etc.) so they rest on squirrel and do not sink under sauce, and add scallion tops. Cover and let simmer 15 minutes. Serves 4 with any vegetable or salad.

RABBIT STEW WITH NOODLES

Follow foregoing recipe, but add enough water to make a thin gravy and when rabbit is nearly done cook in the gravy a package of noodles. Serves 4 with sprinkling of grated Parmesan cheese.

POTTED RABBIT CAMP STYLE

This is a camp dish when trimmings are scarce. If bacon or salt pork is available, cube about a cup of it, fry brown and remove to be returned to pot later. Otherwise use drippings or any available fat into which, when hot, place cut up, floured rabbit to brown. Add salt and pepper, cover with water and let simmer until done. Serve with whatever is available and re-heat left-over for another meal.

RABBIT PAPRIKAS

Anybody who can make Hungarian goulash, the justly famed specialty of many a one-armed joint, or veal paprikas can construct this one, which is much the same, but with rabbit or hare, instead of other meat.

1 rabbit	1 tablespoon paprika
¼ stick butter	water or chicken broth
¼ cup cooking oil	salt and pepper
1 medium onion chopped	½ cup sour cream or more

Saute rabbit in butter and oil until it is brown, add onions and saute until soft. Add paprika, salt and pepper to taste, and water or broth and as liquid cooks down add a little more at a time until rabbit is done, with only a few tablespoons of the liquid remaining. Add sour cream and bring to simmer. Serves 2 or more with buttered noodles.

RABBIT AND SPAGHETTI

1 rabbit	3 tablespoons tomato paste
⅓ cup olive oil	big pinch Italian red pepper
½ pound ham cubed	¼ teaspoon oregano
2 buds garlic chopped	½ teaspoon sugar
1 can, approx. 6 cups	salt to taste
Italian plum tomatoes	1 cup sliced mushrooms

Saute rabbit and ham in olive oil until lightly browned, add garlic and stir, then add all other ingredients except mushrooms which go in for last five minutes. If rabbit is done and sauce still watery, lift out rabbit and return to pot after sauce thickens. Serves three or four over spaghetti with grated Parmesan or Pecorino Romano cheese, and fried cardoon on the side.

SQUIRRELS

BRUNSWICK STEW

No one knows for sure whether Brunswick Stew got its start in Brunswick, Germany; Brunswick, Ga.; or New England and the proper method of preparation is equally controversial. This depends upon the last Brunswick stew cook with whom you discuss putting okra in or leaving it out, the preference in meat that goes into it and a half dozen other points of contention.

It is usually made now with chicken or pork and pork innards, but originally in this country it was put together with small game, usually squirrels, often rabbits, sometimes both—and other things—when available meats and vegetables were used indiscriminately.

6 squirrels	4 medium potatoes cut up
½ stick butter	1 bay leaf
½ cup chopped scallions	⅛ teaspoon thyme
½ cup canned tomatoes	hot red pepper to taste
2 cups green lima beans	salt to taste
2 cups corn cut from cob	water to cover
2 cups sliced okra	2 tablespoons chopped parsley

Cut squirrels in six pieces—forelegs, hindlegs, and across back—and saute in butter until lightly browned, add onions and saute 2 minutes, stirring. Add water to cover squirrels, simmer until they approach doneness and add all other ingredients, cover with water, stir often, simmer into thick mushy stew. Serves 4 or 6 with unsweetened corn bread.

FRIED SQUIRRELS

Select young squirrels or par-boil old cut into six pieces, dip in milk, roll in seasoned flour and fry in hot drippings or vegetable oil until brown and done. To make cup of gravy, pour off cooking fat, reserving about 3 tablespoons and the browned flour from frying squirrels, add ¼ stick butter, two tablespoons flour, one teaspoon chopped chives and one teaspoon chopped parsley, ½ cup chicken broth, ½ cup light cream, salt and pepper and stir over low flame until hot. Serve one or more squirrels and gravy over grits, rice, wild rice or potatoes to each diner, with hot biscuits and guava, grape or currant jelly.

BROILED SQUIRREL

Again, young squirrels if possible. Place whole squirrels over charcoal to broil, basting at start and three or four times during cooking with mixture of ¼ cup olive oil, ¼ cup white wine, I teaspoon lemon juice and add salt and pepper when squirrels are browned and done. Serve one or more squirrels per person with small, new parslied potatoes, field peas, hot biscuits and tart grape jelly.

SQUIRREL AND HEART OF PALM

Canned heart of palm cannot be substituted for the fresh in this dish the way it was made in the old-time Florida hunting camps.

4 or more squirrels	1 cup rice
bacon drippings	1 bay leaf
3 tablespoons flour	salt and pepper
1 small can tomatoes	water to cover
1 large onion	heart of palm

Lightly brown squirrels in bacon drippings or other fat, then add flour to brown, tomatoes, onion, rice, bay leaf, water and a big double handful of heart of palm cut in small chunks and let all simmer until rice is done. Serves 4 or more with hoe cake and coffee.

SQUIRREL WITH WINE

4 squirrels
¼ stick butter
¼ cup olive oil
2 buds garlic crushed
salt and pepper

¼ teaspoon rosemary
1 cup dry white wine
1 cup chicken broth or more
1 tablespoon chopped parsley
2 cups sliced mushrooms

Saute cut up squirrels in butter and oil until lightly browned, add all other ingredidents and simmer until nearly done, turning often. Add parsley and mushrooms to cook five minutes. Serves 4 with the mushrooms and a little sauce spooned over spaghetti and sprinkled with grated cheese, with tossed green salad.

SQUIRREL MULLIGAN

4 squirrels
5 tablespoons flour
½ pound smoked bacon
    cubed
2 medium onions sliced
4 medium potatoes cubed
2 carrots sliced

1 stalk celery and leaves chopped
1 large ripe tomatoes in pieces
4 cups chicken broth
salt to taste
pinch of thyme
dash or two of Tabasco

Brown bacon, remove and set aside. Brown squirrels in drippings, add flour and brown, then onions and saute 2 minutes. Add broth and simmer 20 minutes, then add all other ingredients, including bacon. Simmer until vegetables are done and serve 4 with white bread or rolls and a salad.

SEE RABBIT RECIPES

In addition to the foregoing recipes, squirrel may be prepared in the same way as the several dishes for rabbit, except that the ones requiring marinades are not recommended.

CHAPTER 3

BIG GAME

Deer, Moose, Elk, Caribou and Bear

At a hunting and fishing camp where we served as cook for a time there was this venison—

About 30 feet outside the kitchen door stood a tree laden with McIntosh apples and a few feet beyond, over a knoll, a birch stump salt lick. A half dozen whitetail doe and one spike buck congregated at dusk each evening to feast on the apples we shook out of the tree and on vegetable peelings we put out to keep the diet varied.

Sitting in the kitchen, as hunting season approached, we practiced dry firing on that tender young apple-fed buck silhouetted against the light of the night sky, and we mentally sauted back strip in butter, broiled some chops, roasted a haunch and built a kettle of venison chile con carne.

It was our intention to shoot from inside the kitchen through the open door, taking plenty of time and making one shot from this close range count.

But on the day set for the bagging of the venison we drove down the mountain trail to the village for supplies, got ourselves inadvertently delayed in a saloon and have wondered ever since if some ignoramus without proper appreciation for hand-fed venison got our tender spike buck.

Either that or the musketry of opening day frightened him off to the farthest ridges and he never came back.

The point is that this buck, felled with a single shot, dressed out soon thereafter and aged for a week or ten days at about 38 degrees would have been selected prime venison, of which not a great deal ever reaches the table. It is common practice to shoot what you see in the woods and too often the deer is too old. Diet also has much to do with taste and texture of any meat.

Old venison takes long cooking, like any other meat, and it still will be dry and less than excellent fare.

The white-tailed deer is by far the most numerous, being found in most states, and the mule deer are next. Elk can be had only in the West, but like moose and caribou, from the North, are excellent eating if reasonably young and properly prepared.

VENSION

Specifically, venison should be cooked to about the same doneness as good beef so there will be at least some juicy pink in the center, if you don't care for it rare. Meat from old animals and the tougher cuts will be tenderized somewhat by standing before cooking in a marinade.

Best preparations from the various cuts of venison follow:

Neck—Put through food chopper;

Shoulder—Bone and tie, marinate or use plain for roasting, pot-roasting, stewing or put through food chopper;

Flank—Marinate or plain for stewing, or put through food chopper;

Ribs—Cut into chops;

Hind legs—Roast, pot roast, steaks, stew, or put through food chopper;

Saddle—Roast;

Loin—Broiled steaks;

Backstrip—Saute, broil or roast;

Liver, brains—Prepare as from domesticated animals.

VENISON ROAST

With a larding needle and strips of salt pork or bacon cut ¼ inch thick, lard a saddle roast lengthwise through the filet once on each side and lard a leg roast with strips about three inches apart. Cover the roast with strips of the salt pork or bacon. Put roast on rack in roasting pan, with rib

ends down, if the roast is a saddle, then place in oven pre-
heated to 475 degrees. After 10 minutes reduce heat to 375
and in cooking time allow about 15 minutes to the pound.
Remove salt pork or bacon when it becomes crisp. After 20
minutes of cooking add ½ cup canned beef broth or venison broth made with trimmings and baste roast frequently
thereafter with liquid and drippings, adding a little more
broth as needed. When roast is cooked as desired, move
from pan to warm place, spoon most of the drippings off of
the liquid and spoon a little liquid on each slice of venison.

A roast leg should be carved as you would lamb or ham.
Saddle should be sliced parallel to the bone. Currant jelly,
mint jelly or mint sauce may accompany venison with the
natural gravy, along with vegetables and salad of your choice,
and hot buttered bread or rolls.

VENISON STEAKS AND CHOPS

Coat each side with olive oil and broil quickly under hot
broiler or over charcoal. Serve with accompaniments as
above and triple thick bacon.

BACKSTRIP SAUTE

Heat an iron skillet until a drop of water dances in it
and quickly evaporates. Put a third of a stick of butter in
the skillet, swirl it around and immediately lay in strips
from the backstrip—choicest part of venison—cut a half inch
thick. Let saute a minute, turn and cook to desired degree
of doneness, but in any case with some pink through the
middle. Remove to bowl, add a cup of water or stock to
skillet, salt and pepper, let reduce a moment and pour on
venison.

To complete this meal, Craig Wood, the former National
Open and Masters Golf Champion, does as good a job
as anybody. A native of the Adirondacks and owner of a
fishing and hunting camp in the Catskills, Wood boils potatoes, then sloshes some of the gravy over them at the table,
heats up canned asparagus and loads it with butter, slices
tomatoes and sprinkles with vinegar and bakes up a batch of
biscuits. He also uses venison for bait when trout-fishing.

BUTTER-FRIED VENISON

Doug Bury, operator of Antrim Lodge at Roscoe, N. Y.,
in the heart of the Catskill trout, grouse and deer country,

says venison to be really appreciated should be cooked in camp over an open fire. Moreover, he says, that the way he cooks it produces so much smoke from burning butter that if you cooked it indoors some busybody probably would summon the fire department.

You heat a spider, or iron skillet, over an open wood fire until it is about as hot as it can be, then put in enough butter so that it is about 2 inches deep—and that's where the smoke of burning butter sets in, causing bystanders to start backing off.

Drop tender cuts of salted and peppered venison into the bubbling butter and cook it the way you prefer it, but not too done, turning it once. This is much like Craig Wood's way of doing it in the previous recipe, except that Bury uses much more butter and the butter must burn some or the meat ain't fit to eat.

Ragout means stew and in the preparation of venison in this manner Luchow's, one of the world's most famous German restaurants, rarely has been challenged since opening before the turn of the century. Theodore Roosevelt, a ubiquitous outdoorsman, among other things, was a fancier of the game dishes, especially venison, at the New York restaurant and generally enjoyed with his meal a bottle of Pommard. The two following recipes are among Luchow specialties.

VENISON RAGOUT

4 pounds venison shoulder	2 bay leaves
2 onions, sliced	2 tablespoons beef suet
2 carrots, sliced	vinegar and red wine to cover
6 peppercorns	1 cup red wine
1 tablespoon salt	2 or 3 tablespoons flour

Cut venison into 1½ inch cubes and place in crock. Add equal amounts of vinegar and wine to cover along with onions, carrots, peppercorns, salt and bay leaves. Cover and let stand in refrigerator 1 week. Drain meat and place in very hot roasting pan in which beef suet has been melted. Brown meat 20 or 30 minutes in oven pre-heated to 475 to 500. Add onions and carrots from the marinade, but not the marinade·liquid. Instead, add 1 cup red wine and enough water to cover venison. Lower oven heat to 350, or just hot enough to simmer liquid in pan, and cook 2½ to 3 hours. Place venison on hot dish, remove any excess fat and stir enough flour into pan to make a smooth gravy. Bring to a boil on top of stove, stir thoroughly and strain over venison. Serves 8 with noodles, boiled turnips, kale and chestnuts or green peas, a knob celery salad and a crisp rye bread or rolls.

The other Luchow specialty:

VENISON STEW WITH POTATO DUMPLINGS

4 pounds venison shoulder	6 peppercorns
4 tablespoons butter	2 cloves
4 tablespoons flour	1 bay leaf
1½ teaspoons salt	juice ½ lemon
2 cups stock or bouillon	½ cup red wine
4 cups hot water	potato dumplings
1 small onion, sliced	

Brown the flour in the butter and add salt, stock, hot water, stir and mix well. Add onion, peppercorns, cloves, bay leaf and lemon juice and simmer five minutes. Add venison cut in serving sized pieces. Cover pot and boil 1½ hours. Mix in wine and continue cooking 15 minutes. Serve with potato dumplings (see chapter on Breads, stuffings and side dishes) and other side dishes as for Venison Ragout.

ROAST MARINATED SHOULDER

Bone and tie the shoulder. Place in crock, cover with marinade, cover crock and let stand in refrigerator up to 1 week. Roast 10 minutes in oven preheated to 475 degrees and another 1½ to 2 hours at 425, basting with strained marinade, and occasionally a little venison or beef broth. Serve with a gravy and accompanying side dishes from other venison recipes.

COUNTRY STYLE VENISON STEW

½ pound bacon or salt pork	2 medium potatoes in 1 inch cubes
2 pounds venison steak	
4 tablespoons flour	1 dozen small white onions
6 cups water or beef stock	salt and pepper
1 large tomato, chopped	1 tablespoon chopped parsley
2 medium carrots, sliced	1 cup fresh green peas
2 medium stalks celery, sliced	

Cut bacon into 1 inch cubes and saute in large saucepan until lightly browned. Remove and set aside. Cut venison into 1½ or 2 inch pieces and brown over high flame in 4 tablespoons bacon drippings. Stir in flour, lower flame and let brown 2 or three minutes, stirring several times. Add liquid and let simmer 1 hour or until venison begins to get tender, adding more liquid as necessary. Add all other ingredients, except peas, and continue to simmer to make thick stew. Simmer peas until done in separate pan, strain and spoon over or around stew when served to 4 or 5 with buttered corn muffins or biscuits and a salad.

VENISON SAUSAGE

3 pounds venison	1 teaspoon freshly ground pepper
1 pound smoked ham	
½ pound bacon	1 teaspoon salt or more
1½ teaespoon sage, or more	cayenne to taste
1 teaspoon thyme	

Cut meat in pieces and after mixing with all other ingredients put through fine blade of chopper twice. Form into 3-inch patties ½ inch thick. Pan-fry or broil and serve for breakfast with fried or scrambled eggs, hot biscuits and marmalade or jelly or for dinner with usual accompaniments. Patties also may be wrapped uncooked in tinfoil or wax paper and stored in freezer.

CHILI CON CARNE

1 pound pinto beans	5 cloves garlic chopped
3 pounds chopped venison	6 tablespoons chili powder
4 tablespoon flour	1 tablespoon cumin seed
⅓ cup drippings	2 teaspoons salt or more
1 medium onion, chopped	cayenne or Tabasco to taste

Wash beans and soak overnight. Put on to simmer in water to cover by an inch or so. In large skillet lightly brown venison in drippings and add onions, garlic and flour to saute a few more minutes. Stir several times. Add to beans and cook together until nearly done, adding water as necessary and a half hour before bean and venison mixture is done add other ingredients and cook to medium thick consistency. Serve 8 with scallions and celery hearts and still more poured over rice or spaghetti, the latter known far and wide as Chili-Mac.

VENISON CURRY

¼ cup cooking oil	1 teaspoon salt
2 pounds venison filet	2 tablespoons lemon juice
1 minced medium onion	¼ teaspoon black pepper
1 minced clove garlic	½ cup water or more
2 tablespoons curry powder	⅓ cup grated coconut

Over high flame saute venison cut in ½ inch strips 1 minute on each side; lower flame and add onion and garlic to saute a minute or so, then add all other ingredients and simmer only briefly until it thickens. Serves 4 with white rice, chutney, and side dishes of dried grated orange peel, chopped parsley, chopped nuts, shredded coconut and other final touches to be sprinkled on as desired.

SPAGHETTI AND VENISON MEAT BALLS

Among many Italians, meat sauce does not mean sauce with chopped meat in it, but a sauce flavored with two or three kinds of meat in whole pieces along with meat balls. The meat may be a piece of pork, a piece of lamb and a piece of beef—or any one or two of them—along with a fresh pig's foot and meat balls of beef or beef and pork chopped together. Venison is prepared the same way.

The meat balls:

1 pound venison	1 tablespoon chopped parsley
½ pound pork	1 egg
1 tablespoon grated Parmesan	⅓ cup bread crumbs
salt and pepper	¼ cup olive oil

Put venison and pork through food chopper and mix with other ingredients, except olive oil. Shape mixture into meat balls 1½ to 2 inches in size and brown lightly in the olive oil along with a couple of pork, lamb or venison chops, or a piece of beef. Set the meat balls and other meat aside in a dish.

The sauce:

2 buds garlic, minced	2 teaspoons salt or to taste
6 cups canned plum tomatoes	½ teaspoon basil
pinch of Italian red pepper	1 fresh pig's foot

Saute garlic in oil in which meat and meat balls had been browned. Put tomatoes through sieve and add along with other ingredients and meat, except meat balls which should be returned to pot for last 15 minutes of simmering. Entire cooking time about 1½ hours. Serves 4 or more with spaghetti and grated Parmesan, fried cardoons on the side. Note: After an hour of cooking, if sauce tastes acidity, add a pinch of bicarbonate of soda.

HUNTER'S PIE

2 pounds venison	1 small onion chopped
½ pound smoked ham	2 teaspoons parsley chopped
salt and freshly	pinch of rosemary
ground pepper	1 small bay leaf
flour to dredge	5 cups mashed potatoes, about
¼ stick butter	2 eggs

Cut venison steak or filet into cubes, sprinkle with salt and pepper, dredge in flour and saute in butter with ham cut in smaller cubes until brown. Add onion to saute a minute, then water to cover, adding more as necessary, to simmer venison until done, meantime adding parsley, rosemary and bay leaf. Line sides but not bottom of casserole with mashed potatoes into which the 2 eggs have been whipped along with a little butter and seasoning. Place in hot oven for a few minutes to set, then fill casserole with stew and cover with layer of mashed potatoes and brown in hot oven. A meal in itself for 4 or 5.

VENISON SCALOPPINE WITH MARSALA

⅓ cup olive oil	½ cup slivered prosciutto
2 pounds venison filet	½ pound sliced mushrooms
salt and pepper	¼ cup marsala or sherry
flour to dredge meat	¼ cup beef or chicken broth
1 tablespoon butter	¼ teaspoon oregano

Cut venison into 10 or 12 pieces, pound thin as for veal scaloppine, salt and pepper, dredge in flour and brown on each side in hot olive oil. Move venison to warm plate and discard olive oil, leaving about 1 tablespoon in skillet. Add butter and prosciutto, which should be in strips about twice the size of a matchstick. Let saute a minute over very low flame and add mushrooms which have been blanched and drained. Saute 2 or 3 minutes, stirring. Return venison to skillet, add all other ingredients and simmer 2 or 3 minutes. Garnish with parsley and serve 4 or 5 with spaghetti, butter and cheese sauce, a tossed green salad and hot garlic bread.

VENISON MINCEMEAT

Mincemeat has been a staple in England longer than 'arf and 'arf and in New England since days of the earliest settlers as prepared with venison by housewives, each with her own recipe. This one comes from Mrs. Jean Randolph, of Greenfield, Mass., who has hunted deer and cooked them, too.

3 pounds venison
1 pound beef suet
3 pounds apples
1 pound raisins
1 pound currants
1 tablespoon cinnamon
1 tablespoon salt
1 tablespoon cloves (pow.)
2 teaspoons black pepper

2 teaspoons nutmeg
2 teaspoons alspice
2 cups dark molasses
3 cups brown sugar
juice of 4 lemons and grated rinds
1 quart port wine
½ pint rum

Put venison through food chopper and simmer 1 hour in barely enough water to cover, and let most of liquid cook away toward finish. Put suet and raisins through food chopper. Add to venison along with all other ingredients, including cored, but unpeeled apples finely hand-chopped. Simmer 1 hour stirring often. Put in stone crock or in bottles for pies as game dinner dessert.

KENTUCKY BURGOO

Like Brunswick Stew, Kentucky Burgoo is a dish which in pioneer days was made with any available meat and vegetables. Burgoo differs from Brunswick Stew in the omission of okra, the use of more tomatoes, and the addition of cabbage. In both dishes squirrels and rabbits as well as venison and birds were among the ingredients in early days, now supplanted by beef and chicken. A modernized version with old-time overtones follows:

2 pounds venison steak	2 cups canned tomatoes
1 pheasant or other birds	2 sliced carrots
1 pound potatoes diced	corn cut from 2 ears
3 cups chopped cabbage	2 teaspoons salt
½ cup chopped onions	red pepper to taste

Cut venison into 1 inch cubes and simmer with disjointed pheasant, frying chicken or other fowl until latter is done. While venison continues to simmer, bone the fowl and cut into chunks. When venison has cooked about 1 hour, add all other ingredients and when nearly done return pieces of fowl to pot and, adding water as necessary, cook into soupy stew. Serves 6 with waterground meal corn cakes and a green salad.

OTHER VENISON RECIPES

In the chapter on Small Game will be found several recipes which may be converted from rabbit and squirrel by using equivalent amount of venison.

These include, Rabbit Creole, Rabbit Paprikas, Rabbit with Sawmill Gravy, Squirrel with Heart of Palm, Squirrel Mulligan, etc.

BEAR

Once so plentiful as to be a nuisance in some areas, bears are becoming increasingly scarce over most of the United States with the result that few devotees of game cookery get a chance to prepare this meat which some regard as excellent and others shun as tough, stringy and unsavory. The animal's age has much to do with the quality of the meat. Diet can be a factor and still another is whether the animal is a male killed during rutting season or a nursing sow.

The cooking time required will depend much upon age

of the animal and size of the meat—as in all cookery—but, in any case, bear, like pork, should be well done with no trace of pink and, also like pork, it will not require larding or strips of fat placed over it, known as barding.

BEAR STEAKS, CHOPS AND ROASTS

If the animal is young, proceed as you would with young venison or beef. After proper aging, rub with a little oil and broil the steaks or chops. Old meat and tough cuts may be soaked in a marinade then wiped dry and cooked as desired.

Roasts should be merely salted and peppered and placed in an oven set at 400 degrees for 15 minutes, then cooked 20 minutes to the pound at 350 degrees, with frequent basting from pan drippings and a little water added occasionally. This can be thickened with flour at the finish for gravy.

If the roast is marinated, use some of the marinade and water for basting.

Serve with sweet potatoes, apple sauce or apple butter, the sweet potatoes cooked in with the roast toward the finish, if no marinade is used. Any vegetables fit in well, along with hot bread.

BRAISED BEAR AND SWEET POTATOES

4 pounds bear steak	1 chopped stalk celery
1 minced clove garlic	5 raw sweet potatoes
1 minced small onion	salt and pepper

Cut meat into 2 inch cubes and brown in drippings or vegetable oil on top of stove. Transfer to Dutch oven or roasting pan with lid. Add just enough water to prevent sticking, about ⅓ cup (and a little from time to time during cooking), cover tightly and place in pre-heated 350-degree oven with 1 minced clove garlic, 1 minced medium onion, 1 chopped small stalk celery. When meat begins to get tender add sweet potatoes sliced lengthwise and a little more water as necessary. Cover and continue cooking until meat and potatoes are done.

BEAR HASH

In old-time camps, when bears were plentiful, breakfast sometimes consisted of a hash made of left-over cooked bear meat mixed with ½ the amount of chopped boiled potatoes and a little onion all browned lightly together in bacon drippings.

CHAPTER 4

UPLAND GAME BIRDS

Quail, Grouse, Turkey, Woodcock, Dove and Pheasant

Perhaps his size works against him because we expect our monarchs to be something out of the ordinary in stature and general robust appearance, but the quail could qualify as the champion of American game birds, both for the sport he provides in the field and the succulence at the table.

He weighs less than a half pound, contrasted with as much as 20 pounds for a turkey gobbler and nearly two pounds for a ruffed grouse, which two generally share the title of champion. But neither of these latter affords better shooting —nor better food—than Bob White and his half dozen near kin scattered about the country.

The turkey and the grouse also are lacking in sportsmanship. With a quick veer, both of them will maneuver in flight instinctively to put a tree or a thicket between themselves and the hunter to avoid getting a charge of shot in the rump. Not the quail. Bob White goes off pretty much in a straight line, or at a true angle without guile, but is still easier missed than hit.

This most popular member of the quail family is at home in the Southern pine flats and palmetto scrub, and is raised commercially for market. He is regarded unanimously as one of the finest of all birds to hunt, because of the comparative ease with which the covey generally can be located by good pointers and setters, their natural tendency to hold, rather than flush or run, and finally the speed with which the covey gets away when they take off.

Older birds can be tough and require longer moist cooking, but, on the whole, there is no finer eating than this white meat flavored by the grass and plant seeds and the berries that make up the main part of the diet. They may be prepared much the same as any white-meated fowl, including the chicken, but they have enough of the flavor of the outdoors to fit better with outdoor side accompaniments than does a barnyard habitue.

All other quail in this country—and there are five genera divided further into sub-species—are regarded well as game food in the widely scattered localities where they are found.

A brace of quail generally make a portion, although a real quail-eater will wade through many more, whereas one grouse, also white-meated and fine eating, generally is a meal for one, and like quail, grouse come in many varieties.

The wild turkey is, of course, regarded as one of the real prizes of hunting, due to their wariness, speed of flight, size and important place in tradition. They are not as abundant as some game, but still supply more than 400,000 dinners a year.

Among smaller birds, the woodcock and dove share about equal billing as delicacies, and the pheasant, white-meated and about the size of a fryer, comes closest of all to being barnyard poultry.

For other birds, such as the crow, for example, whose flesh is as dark and dry as his feathers and tougher than an anvil, we have no recipes.

Upland game birds should be dry-plucked, not scalded and never skinned, then rinsed off and dried. The cook should also bear in mind the dryness of most game birds because of little fat due to outdoor activity and a rough way of life compared with their indolent, self-satisfied, well-tended and well-fed barnyard kinfolks.

Secure bacon or salt pork strips across the breast or baste when dry cooking, such as roasting, these birds whose succulence is governed somewhat by diet. Quail of all kinds subsist mainly on grass and weed seeds and berries; woodcock shun nearly everything but earthworms; doves and pigeons favor seeds, berries, grain and nuts, including some acorns;

grouse will eat all kinds of seeds, buds and insects and upwards of 400 different items have been found in the diet of
the ruffed grouse; pheasants prefer grain, but will eat berries,
fruits and such, and the wild turkey thrives on a cross-
section of the above, depending upon locale.

Allow two or more smaller birds (quail, etc.) per portion,
one grouse for one or two portions, a pheasant for two or
more. Servings from a turkey depends upon its size, which
infrequently will be as much as 20 pounds, with the average
around 12 to 15 pounds.

For roasting, truss all game birds as you would barnyard
fowl.

QUAIL

QUAIL ON TOAST

Sprinkle birds inside and out with salt and pepper, spread
on butter with fingers to cover each bird and put a pat of
butter inside each. Arrange breastside up in baking pan with
a half-stick of butter for, say, a dozen quail. Place in oven
pre-heated to 375 degrees for 10 minutes, after which spoon
over birds 3 or 4 tablespoons of hot chicken broth or water
combined with butter. Lower the oven to 325 and after 5
minutes baste again. In another 10 minutes baste again and
they should be done.

Remove quail to slices of lightly buttered toast on hot
plates, add to the pan a teaspoon of lemon juice, a couple of
pats of butter, a half cup of broth or water and simmer on
top of stove stirring. Add pepper and salt if needed and
spoon a tablespoon or two of sauce from the pan over the
birds and toast. Serve with wild rice, grits or small boiled
potatoes, field peas, orange or grapefruit marmalade, guava
or grape jelly and any simple chilled salad.

STUFFED QUAIL

Stuffing is advocated by some fanciers of quail, but there
isn't much room for it in so small a bird. Anything that
strikes your fancy may be used, such as two or three oysters
simmered until nearly done, two or three green olives of the
kind stuffed with whole almonds, chopped truffles, or two or
three mushroom caps and in each instance ingredient to be
mixed with buttered bread crumbs, a little chopped parsley
and celery leaves and partly cooked, except olives which
should be merely heated. (See chapter on other stuffings.)

Having stuffed your quail proceed as in recipe for quail on toast, but skewer the opening shut, with a toothpick to prevent stuffing from falling out. Accompany with side dishes recommended for quail on toast, plus hot biscuits.

BROILED QUAIL

Quail may be broiled whole or split down the back and flattened and they may be broiled under a stove broiler or over coals. In either case they should be lightly brushed with a good cooking oil, preferably, or butter and turned often to prevent burning during the 15 minutes or less needed to get them done. Two or three strips of slowly fried, crisp bacon fits in well with broiled quail along with the other side dishes mentioned for quail on toast.

FRIED QUAIL

Salt and pepper quail inside and out, roll in flour and fry in very hot deep cooking oil until they begin to brown. Lower heat and continue to fry until well-browned. Serve with French fried potatoes, collard, mustard or turnip greens (all obtainable frozen), a tart jelly and hot biscuits.

POTTED QUAIL

This recipe is equally adaptable to grouse or chukkar and is the method of preparing game birds popularized by Mrs. Charles Dickey, wife of the nationally famous outdoorsman.

8 quail	water
salt and pepper	6 large mushrooms, sliced
flour	2 tablespoons chopped parsley
¼ cup butter	buttered toast

Sprinkle salt and pepper on quail inside and out, lightly flour and brown in butter. Add mushrooms and ½ cup of water. Cover and cook 10 minutes over low heat. Add parsley, cover and cook 10 more minutes or a little longer, turning them occasionally. Salt and pepper sauce to taste and spoon over quail on toast.

QUAIL PATTI

This is an improvisation, played strictly by ear, but it turned out to be an epicurean melody created jointly by Mrs. Art Smith, wife of the outdoor writer, and Mrs. Red Smith, wife of the syndicated sports columnist, and it is now a popular dish in New York quail circles.

8 quail	juice of 6 oranges
salt and pepper	pinch of thyme
flour	6 thin slices of lemon
1 stick of butter	3 tablespoons currant jelly
5 sliced·mushrooms	water

Salt and pepper quail inside and out, lightly flour and brown in skillet in butter. Move quail to baking pan and saute mushrooms in skillet. Add mushrooms and butter from skillet to quail along with orange juice, thyme, lemon slices and ¼ cup of water. Bake ½ hour or a little longer, turning quail occasionally. Add currant jelly to sauce and serve with wild rice.

SMOTHERED QUAIL

8 quail	2½ cups canned chicken broth
salt and pepper	pinch of thyme
½ cup cubed bacon	½ bay leaf
6 tablespoons flour	1 tablespoon chopped parsley
2 scallions and tops minced	
1 tablespoon minced celery leaves	

Saute bacon until brown and remove from skillet. Put lightly peppered and salted quail in drippings and when browned remove and add flour to brown, then onions and stir a minute. Add all other ingredients and return bacon and quail to gravy, cover and simmer 20 or 30 minutes turning occasionally until done. Add more chicken broth if needed. Serve with white rice, whole hominy or grits, snap beans or field peas, biscuits or corn bread and fried tomatoes.

QUAIL AND CABBAGE

8 quail
salt and pepper
4 strips of bacon
4 cups cabbage

12 small white onions
12 small new potatoes
1 cup of water, or more
pinch of red pepper

Cut bacon into about six pieces, slowly fry until crisp and remove from saucepan. Salt and pepper quail and saute until brown in the drippings and set aside. Slice about 5 cups of cabbage thin as possible and brown lightly in the drippings. Add onions, potatoes, water and pepper, return quail to the saucepan, cover and let all simmer until potatoes are nearly done. Uncover and let simmer until most of water has evaporated. Serve with bacon pieces as garnish.

QUAIL AND CHERRIES

8 quail
pepper
⅓ stick of butter
2 tablespoons brandy
¼ cup white wine

1 cup of stock or water
24 canned black cherries
¼ cup syrup from cherries
½ teaspoon grated lemon rind
1 teaspoon lemon juice

Salt and pepper quail and roast in oven until well-browned. Add brandy, wine and water and continue cooking 10 or 12 minutes turning several times. Remove quail to hot plates, strain sauce into small saucepan, add cherries, cherry syrup, lemon rind and lemon juice, and a little more stock or water if needed. Simmer until cherries are warmed through. Spoon sauce over quail and place cherries around birds, and on side glazed small white onions, green peas and a baked potato with butter, a trace of sour cream and sprinkling of chives.

QUAIL AND CREAMED CELERY

8 quail
salt and pepper
2 cups water or stock
4 tablespoons flour
½ stick butter
1 tablespoon minced onion

1 cup chopped celery
  and leaves
⅓ cup sherry
1 cup light cream
1 teaspoon chopped parsley

Salt and pepper quail and brown lightly in butter. Move to casserole. Saute onions a minute or so over low flame. Add flour and mix without browning. Add to quail the onion flour and butter mixture and all other ingredients, cover and bake in 350 degree oven 25 or 30 minutes, adding more stock or water as necessary and salt and pepper to taste. Serve with wild rice, green peas and corn sticks.

QUAIL WITH GRAPES AND ALMONDS

8 quail
salt and pepper
flour
⅓ stick butter

¼ cup white wine
1 cup small white grapes
1 cup water or stock
4 tablespoons sliced almonds

Salt and pepper quail and roll in flour. Saute in butter until browned. Add wine and water and let simmer 15 minutes turning several times. Add salt and pepper to taste and grapes. Swirl to warm grapes. Shut off heat. Move quail to hot plates, spoon sauce over them and arrange grapes around quail. Spoon over each a half tablespoon of sliced almonds which have been lightly browned in butter. Serve with buttered wild rice which includes a few mushrooms, small green buttered lima beans, a sliced cucumber salad and corn sticks.

WOODCOCK

Quail are the most abundant of game birds, both wild in their several varieties raised in captivity to be released for the gunner and sold for market. Thus the foregoing recipes call for quail, but woodcock, doves and grouse may be prepared the same way and some of the recipes will fit pheasants and a small turkey.

Requiring a skilled gunner to bring them down and not overly plentiful, woodcock are a rare delicacy—described by many as the finest eating among all game birds. Purchased from import markets, the price comes high. Two of them make a good portion, but three or more will be done away with by a hungry hunter. The simpler they are prepared the better, and roasting or broiling—as you would quail—are the most popular woodcock dishes.

DEEP-FRIED WOODCOCK

Lightly salt and pepper whole birds and deep fry four or five minutes in smoking hot salad oil or olive oil. There should be enough oil to cover them entirely and it should be very hot. Pick them up and eat them, without the bother of cutting them into pieces. Corn sticks, hash-browned or French fried potatoes and a preferred vegetable make good accompaniments.

WOODCOCK IN CASSEROLE

8 woodcock	pinch of thyme
½ stick butter	1 tablespoon parsley
⅓ cup chopped scallions	1½ cup wild rice
and tops	1 bay leaf
⅓ cup chopped celery	salt and pepper
and tops	2½ cups canned chicken broth
1 clove garlic	¼ cup sherry

Lightly brown woodcocks in butter, turning often, and while so doing thoroughly wash wild rice, boil five minutes, wash and let drain in sieve. Add scallions and tops, chopped, garlic and celery tops to browned birds and let saute a minute, then move all this and birds to casserole. Put all other ingredients, including wild rice, into pot in which birds were browned, bring to simmer and pour over birds in casserole. Cover and cook 20 to 30 minutes in 350 degree oven. Uncover and cook, stirring occasionally, until the stock has been absorbed, 10 or 15 minutes. Serve from casserole with steamed buttered broccoli with a few drops of lemon juice, green peas or baby lima beans and hot rolls.

DOVES

There is so little difference between doves and pigeons that to name one is to identify the other for purposes of preparing a meal. Both are on the dry side, but nonetheless tasty, the favorite game of many outdoorsmen. The young birds, quickly cooked and frequently basted or covered with strips of bacon are as good as any roasted, but are especially adapted to wet cooking.

POTTED DOVES AND DUMPLINGS

This dish is identical with the recipe for rabbit stew and dumplings, which see. Six or eight doves will be required. If fewer birds are used, cut down on the ingredients.

DOVE PILAU

Call it Pilau, Jambalaya, Pilaf, Paella, Arroz, Risotto or by any other name and rice comes out pretty much the same when cooked with meat or sea food in broth. There are variations, with or without tomatoes or saffron, for example, but the dish one way or another is good and doves fit this one.

6 doves	pinch of thyme
4 oz. cubed bacon	1 bay leaf
1 medium onion	salt and Tabasco to taste
1½ cups rice	1 tablespoon parsley
5 cups canned chicken broth	¼ pound button mushrooms

Fry bacon over low fire until lightly browned, add doves and brown, then onions to saute a moment. Add all other ingredients, bring to boil and add thoroughly washed, uncooked rice, cover and cook slowly until rice is tender and broth absorbed, stirring once. Stir in mushrooms to cook three or four minutes. This is a meal in itself with a salad.

GROUSE

Most of the numerous species of grouse rate high on the list of delicacies among game birds. When roasted they require a covering of bacon strips or frequent basting. Overcooking will make them dry.

GROUSE AMANDINE

4 grouse	1 tablespoon lemon juice
1 stick of butter or more	salt and pepper
½ cup sliced almonds	chopped parsley

Rub birds inside and out with butter, sprinkle on salt and pepper and roast in pre-heated 400 degree oven 30 minutes, basting with melted butter and lemon juice. Move to warm plate, add ½ cup water to roasting pan and bring to boil on top of stove. Strain sauce into skillet in which almonds have been lightly browned in butter. Season to taste and pour over birds. Garnish with parsley. Serve with braised celery, green peas, cranberry sauce and buttered toast.

ROAST STUFFED GROUSE

Select a stuffing from the chapter on Breads and Stuffings. Stuff grouse loosely, close vent with skewers or thread and proceed with roasting as in foregoing, except pre-heat oven to 400 degrees and after 10 minutes turn down to 350 and cook until done, 20 or 25 minutes. Again, serve with cranberry sauce, especially if a sage stuffing is used. (As for sage, be careful of sage hens, a species of grouse which feeds largely on sage and may be so strong of it as to be repellent at the table.)

PHEASANT

Pheasant is much like chicken and the least wild-tasting of all game birds, due in part to its diet of corn, peas and such. Thus pheasant may be prepared in the same way as other upland game or as barnyard fowl, and will require about the same cooking time as the latter. It comes down to a matter of age and size, which can be controlled to assure quality if the pheasant is purchased at the market, rather than shot in the field.

ROAST PHEASANT

A 2 pound pheasant will require about 35 minutes to roast unstuffed and a little longer with a stuffing listed in the chapter on Breads and Stuffings.

PHEASANT CACCIATORE

This dish is seldom encountered in American restaurants, but often is part of a holiday feast in an Italian home, with the sauce from the pheasant over spaghetti, and on the side roast young goat, hot sausages sauted with garlic and perhaps mushrooms in olive oil, fried breaded cardoon, broccoli with lemon juice, eggplant Parmigiana, all preceded by an antipasto and followed by finochio, fruit, nuts, cheese, Italian pastry and espresso and anisette. Then supper.

1 2-½-pound pheasant	2 tablespoons tomato paste
½ cup olive oil	1 teaspoon salt
1 chopped medium onion	pinch Italian red pepper
2 minced cloves garlic	1 teaspoon oregano
3 cups canned plum tomatoes	2 tablespoons chopped parsley

Disjoint pheasant and saute in olive oil until brown. Put the tomatoes through a sieve and add with all other ingredients. Simmer slowly until pheasant is done, about 30 minutes. Remove pheasant and let sauce continue cooking for an hour. Return pheasant to pot to reheat. Serve with spaghetti, about 3 portions.

BROILED PHEASANT

Split young pheasant lengthwise, rub with olive oil and, turning several times, broil, preferably over charcoal, until brown and done. Olive oil, rather than butter, is recommended for open fire cooking.

For a finishing barbecue touch, the recipe for sauce used with spareribs on President Lyndon B. Johnson's Texas ranch works as well with pheasant, spread on both sides of the halved bird for the last half minute or so of cooking.

¼ cup chopped onion	¼ cup vinegar
¼ cup butter	¼ cup catsup
¼ cup lemon juice	¼ cup Worcestershire sauce

Cook onions in butter until soft, add all other ingredients, simmer five minutes, strain to remove onions and swab on the birds. This is on the tart side and a good variation is omit the vinegar and add 1 teaspoon chili powder. If the birds are old they will require more cooking and after spreading on the sauce, put them in the oven for a half hour or so. French fried potatoes, salad and biscuits go with it.

PHEASANT WITH SWEET CREAM

1 young pheasant	4 tablespoons sherry
4 tablespoons butter	1 pint heavy sweet cream
1 cup water or broth	Salt and freshly ground pepper

Cut pheasant in pieces, brown lightly in butter (using more butter if necessary) add water or chicken broth, and let simmer until liquid is reduced to a few tablespoons. Add sherry, simmer five minutes more, add cream and seasoning to taste and let simmer to thicken.

PHEASANT WITH SOUR CREAM

See recipe for Rabbit Paprikas in chapter on small game.

WILD TURKEY

A roast wild turkey with stuffing—preferably bearing a trace of sage—and cranberry sauce on the side could well be the basis of feasts which caused the gods to rave.

The majestic bird and the tart red berries are a happy coincidence contrived by nature to make them native American and, with a well-seasoned stuffing, to make a meal without need of further embellishment, or, as is generally more likely, suitable for being surrounded with all manner of side dishes. The turkey—and most especially the wild one—is a bird for festive occasions.

Cook the wild one like you would his barnyard relative. Clean, wash, truss, salt and pepper lightly inside and out. Stuff it, sew up the vent, smear it generously with butter and put it in an oven pre-heated to 450 degrees for 15 minutes, then turn the heat to 350. Allow 15 minutes to the pound, basting frequently with a stick of butter mixed with 1 cup dry white wine, three cups of broth, a dash of pepper, a pinch each of thyme and rosemary simmered for 10 minutes before starting the basting.

Suggested stuffings are listed in the chapter on Breads and Stuffings.

To prepare a turkey in any way other than roasting would be desecration. Sandwiches spread with Durkee Famous Dressing, a bottled American sauce on the market since 1857, is about as good a way as any to dispose of any left-over meat the next day.

Or hot dishes may be prepared in a number of ways. The following recipes work equally well with turkey or pheasant.

WILD TURKEY A LA KING

¼ cup butter	2 egg yolks
½ thinly sliced green pepper	2 teaspoons lemon juice
1 cup thinly sliced mush-	½ teaspoon paprika
rooms	3 tablespoons sherry, about
½ cup chicken broth	¼ cup minced pimento
2 tablespoons flour	salt and white pepper
2 cups sweet cream	buttered toast
3 cups cubed turkey	

Saute green pepper in butter for a moment, add canned chicken broth or giblet broth and let simmer another moment. Add mushrooms to simmer a moment, then mix flour with enough chicken stock so it will pour. Shut off heat and add flour mixture slowly, stirring briskly to prevent lumping. Simmer a moment. Shut off heat and add cream, turkey and egg yolks, stirring in, and all other ingredients. Heat but do not boil and serve on buttered toast to six. A border of green peas may be arranged around the edge of the dish and an endive and cucumber salad makes a good accompaniment.

WILD TURKEY TETRAZZINI

3 tablespoons butter	1 tablespoon chopped parsley
3 tablespoons flour	3 cups cubed turkey
1 cup chicken broth	3 tablespoons sherry or more
½ cup sliced mushrooms	salt and white pepper
½ cup sweet cream	grated Parmesan cheese
dash of paprika	½ box spaghetti

In saucepan mix flour and butter, but do not brown. Add broth and mushrooms and simmer until thick. Add all other ingredients, except cheese and spaghetti and when it comes to simmer turn off fire. Meantime boil the spaghetti until done, but firm, drain thoroughly, mix with sauce, place in baking pan, sprinkle on two or three tablespoons cheese, and brown lightly under broiler. A salad similar to the above with Turkey a la King goes good with this.

WILD TURKEY WET-HASH

2 cups cubed potatoes
3 cups cubed turkey
1 small minced onion
4 tablespoons butter
3 tablespoons flour
1 cup chicken stock

pinch of thyme
1 tablespoon chopped
  celery leaves
salt and freshly ground pepper
1 tablespoon chopped parsley

Boil cubed potatoes until done. Meanwhile, brown flour in butter, add onions to saute a minute, then add all other ingredients, including thoroughly drained potatoes. Stir well and let steam over low fire for five minutes. If there is any turkey gravy left-over, omit butter, flour and chicken stock from foregoing and use 1 cup of the gravy.

WILD TURKEY SALAD

2 cups chopped turkey
½ cup mayonnaise
½ cup minced celery

2 teaspoons lemon juice
2 tablespoons chopped parsley
salt and pepper

Mix, chill and make sandwiches or cube, instead of chopping, add same ingredients, mix, chill and serve on lettuce leaves with sweet pickles, cold asparagus spears, thin slices of boiled ham and other items to make a cold plate.

HOT TURKEY SANDWICH

Saute in butter enough turkey for required number of sandwiches and make sandwiches with hot buttered toast spread lightly with sweet relish if desired.

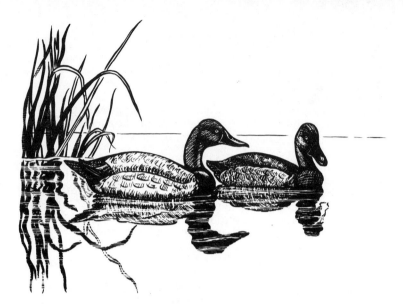

CHAPTER 5

WATERFOWL

Duck, Goose, Snipe and Rail

The Canvasback duck ranks higher with more outdoor gourmets than any other waterfowl, and well it might especially if it has been on a wild celery diet, is reasonably young, dressed and plucked soon after being taken and aged four or five days at around 37 or 38 degrees. The Canvasback is known as the King of Ducks, and is a diving duck as distinguished from the other group of palatable ducks known as the puddle ducks.

From among these latter comes the Canvasback's chief challenger as table fare, the more abundant Mallard, followed by the Black Duck, the Teals, the Widgeons, Redheads, Butterballs and many others. They are all followed by the mergansers, fish ducks, worthless as food.

The Canvasback is a big and noble fellow, with a taste all his own and the picturesqueness of being able to travel above 70 miles an hour when he is high-tailing it out of range of the whistling No. 4 shot. He is bigger than most ducks, weighing upwards of 3 pounds, but when you get one that size he may be 20 or more years of age and couldn't be tenderized in a blast furnace. Somewhat younger ones are what the gourmets rave about.

A mallard will run around two pounds and a teal less than a pound—and hope they are young—all of which is important when you set out to cook a duck so the dark meat will be juicy and tender. Cooking time depends upon size as well as age.

Ducks should be carefully cooked, not only to avoid overcooking but to get it done enough so it won't quack when sliced, contrary to the opinion of those who can't enjoy roast duck unless the blood trickles off the chin of the eater. Not overdone, but not raw either is a pretty good way of putting it.

The Canada goose, Snow Goose, Brant and other geese are handled very much the same as ducks, but in roasting their flavorsome, dark rather dry meat will require more cooking time due to their larger size. They will range between about eight and fifteen pounds, depending upon the species, and hope you get a young one. The old ones can out-tough an old duck, if possible.

Snipe and rails may be prepared in the same fashion as ducks also, but will hardly be as tasty as a prime Canvasback or Mallard and there is nothing to be done about it.

WILD DUCK

In offering recipes for the preparation of waterfowl, there is that obstacle having to do with the fact that wild ducks come in varying sizes ranging through many species. A young Canvasback or Mallard will be larger than an old Teal and cooking time is a matter based on size as well as age.

With the foregoing in mind, the following recipes are based upon the large Canvasback and the home cook must make allowances for smaller ducks.

PLAIN ROAST DUCK

2 ducks	salt and pepper
butter	water

Rub the ducks with butter and place 3 tablespoons of butter in each. Sprinkle inside and out with salt and pepper. Pour over them a scant ¼ cup water and place in over preheated to 400 degrees. Roast 30 minutes or so, basting with a little butter and chicken stock 2 or 3 times. When done, upend the ducks to pour the butter and juices into the pan. Slice breast meat thin and place on hot plates, add a little stock to pan, heat it and spoon a little of the pan juice over the meat and serve 4 with buttered wild rice, green lima beans, currant jelly or marmalade and hearts of lettuce with French dressing.

STUFFED ROAST DUCK

Follow foregoing recipe, but omit butter inside duck and select stuffing from recipes in chapter on Breads and Stuffings.

LARDED ROAST DUCK

Follow either of the two foregoing recipes after larding each side of the breast lengthwise about ½ inch under the skin with larding needle and strip of salt pork.

PRESSED ROAST DUCK

2 ducks	pinch of thyme
2 duck (or chicken) livers	⅓ cup red wine
3 tablespoons butter	1 teaspoon Worcestershire
1 tablespoon flour	salt
few grains nutmeg	freshly ground pepper
1 tablespoon minced onion	2 tablespoons brandy

Saute livers only lightly so they remain rare and remove from skillet, in which brown flour, adding more butter if needed. Add onions and saute a minute. Add other ingredients, except brandy and simmer 4 or 5 minutes, adding a little water or broth if too thick. Add cut up livers and mash all through sieve. Meanwhile, roast ducks as for plain roast duck in foregoing, but not longer than 15 minutes. Remove skin from breasts, slice the breasts ¼ inch thick. Extract juices from duck carcasses with duck press and add to liver sauce in chafing dish. Add 2 tablespoons of brandy and turn slices of duck in simmering sauce 2 or 3 times and serve with the sauce, wild rice and usual game accompaniments. Serves 4.

BROILED DUCK

Split ducks lengthwise, salt and pepper lightly, rub with olive oil and broil about 10 minutes to each side, turning several times to prevent burning. Place on hot plates and pour over duck halves melted butter with a few drops of lemon juice and chopped parsley.

DUCK AND TURNIPS

2 ducks in pieces	1 tablespoon flour
6 turnips	1 small clove minced garlic
3 tablespoons butter	pinch of thyme
12 small white onions	1 teaspoon chopped parsley
4 ounces cubed ham	salt and pepper

Brown pieces of duck in butter and add all other ingredients, except onions. Let saute 10 minutes, stirring often to prevent sticking. Add enough water to fall just short of covering mixture, simmer until done, about ½ hour. Add onions to cook last 15 minutes. Serve with turnip tops boiled separately with bacon, sliced tomatoes with French dressing and hot rolls. Serves 4 or more.

DUCK AND MUSHROOMS

Follow previous recipe, but use ½ pound mushrooms instead of turnips and about ½ the amount of water used with duck and turnips.

DUCK AND SAUERKRAUT

2 ducks in pieces	freshly ground pepper
1 medium onion, chopped	1 pound kraut or more
¼ stick butter	1 teaspoon caraway seed
¼ teaspoon salt	1 cup canned chicken stock

Brown ducks in butter slowly. Add onion and saute until soft. Add all other ingredients, cover and simmer 10 minutes, after which lift duck on top of kraut, which should have been washed in sieve under cold water and squeezed dry. Cover and cook another 20 minutes. Serve with mashed potatoes, apple butter and toasted rye bread. Serves 4.

DUCK AND WHITE BEANS

1 pound white pea beans	2 cloves garlic, minced
2 ducks in pieces	freshly ground black pepper
6 ounces cubed bacon	salt
1 medium onion, chopped	2 teaspoons chopped parsley

Soak beans overnight in water to cover, then simmer gently until nearly done. Brown bacon in skillet and pour off drippings, reserving 3 tablespoons. In this brown pieces of duck and then add onion and garlic to saute until soft. Empty contents of skillet into beans, add salt and pepper and cook until beans are done, stirring in parsley and 2 tablespoons butter a few minutes before serving with white rice, broccoli and lemon juice, apple sauce and hot rolls.

DUCK JAMBALAYA

1 duck in pieces	1 tablespoon chopped celery
6 ounces cubed ham	leaves
3 tablespoons olive oil	2 teaspoons chopped parsley
3 tablespoons butter	4 cups canned chicken stock
1 medium chopped onion	1 bay leaf
1 minced clove garlic	salt and Tabasco
1 sliced green pepper	pinch of thyme
2 cups rice	

Lightly brown duck, cut through bone in small pieces, and ham in olive oil and butter. Add onion, garlic and sweet pepper and saute for a minute or two, stirring. Add all other ingredients, except the rice and simmer 10 minutes. Wash rice in sieve under running water and add to simmering mixture to cook about 15 minutes, until done but still firm. Add more stock, if necessary. Serves 4 with a salad and a vegetable.

GOOSE

When you say goose you are speaking of food that may be as tough and dry as a tin roof under a hot sun. Hence, the hunter who is more interested in the eating quality of game than in the impressive size of it, always selects a target near the end of the flight, where the goslings trail the leaders who through many migrations have built up not only wisdom, but muscle fit to dent a cleaver.

An eight-pound Canada goose generally is both tender and superlatively tasty when roasted. But if your hunter wanted to have his cake—or a gander of majestic proportions—and eat it, too, call for a power saw to do the carving.

ROAST GOOSE

See recipes for plain, larded and stuffed roast duck, but allow 15 minutes per pound in cooking, starting and finishing in 350-degree oven. Stuffings will be found in chapter on Breads, Stuffings and Side Dishes.

OTHER RECIPES

Follow recipes for duck, increasing quantities and cooking time, but, because of the size of a goose and by tradition, it is almost invariably roasted with or without stuffing.

Red cabbage is a fine side dish for most game and almost a must with goose.

SNIPE AND RAIL

Recipes in chapter on Upland Game Birds may be followed for Snipe and Rail, the latter also known as meadow hens, marsh hens and mud hens. When roasting, they invariably should be covered with bacon.

CHAPTER 6

FISH

Salt Water and Fresh

In the whole lexicon of cooking there is no word more comprehensive than "fish," considering that three-fourths of the earth's surface is composed of water. That leaves small room, by comparison, for meat, fruits, vegetables, dairy products, grains and cereals, mixed in with or surrounded by population, mountain peaks, deserts, jungles, and Bar-B-Que joints dedicated to dispensing mediocrity with the promise of no waiting.

Also there is no word more abused on some menus than "fish" in the way they are prepared, but, on the whole, fish suffers less from bad cooking than most items. The main fault to be found is that the fish is not always as fresh as it should be and in too many places it is presented with too little imagination.

In this age of the quick-freeze and an estimated 60,-000,000 sport anglers besides the commercial fisherman, there is no excuse for anything except excellent fish in the home kitchen and the best kind for the dish you plan to cook.

A couple of points to remember: If you buy frozen fish, it should be hard-frozen when you obtain it and without any oiliness or discolor. Fresh fish should be just that and should be selected with care. Pass up shrimp which are beginning to show an off color, lobsters and crabs which are dead, and the general run of fish whose gills are turning grey, and with odor likely to bring on the fumigators.

In the following recipes, where a specific fish is mentioned, this does not mean only that fish is suited to the preparation, but the fish suggested is among the best and any similar fish may be used. For example, the preparation of lobster bisque and shrimp bisque is identical. All chowders are much alike. Oily fish should be broiled and drier fish fried and so on. Most of these dishes can be made in camp or at the seashore as part of a fishing trip.

CHOWDER, BISQUE, GUMBO, ETC.

MANHATTAN CLAM CHOWDER

½ cup cubed bacon	¼ cup chopped celery
½ cup chopped onion	and leaves
¼ cup chopped carrots	1 teaspoon salt
2 cups diced potatoes	⅛ teaspoon pepper
5 cups water	¼ teaspoon thyme
1 cup canned tomatoes	3 doz. chowder clams
1 tablespoon chopped parsley	and juice

Brown bacon in saucepan and pour off drippings except 2 tablespoons. Saute onions lightly, add all other ingredients, except clams, which should be steamed open in separate pot, chopped coarsely and added to the chowder mixture when it is nearly done. The clam liquor should be strained into the chowder through a napkin to remove all sand. Add more water if needed.

COMBINATION CLAM CHOWDER

Follow above recipe and just before serving add ½ cup heavy cream.

BOSTON CLAM CHOWDER

½ cup cubed bacon	⅛ teaspoon pepper
½ cup sliced onion	3 doz. chowder clams
3 cups cubed potatoes	and juice
4 cups scalded milk	½ cup cream
1 teaspoon salt	2 tablespoons butter

Brown bacon and pour off drippings except 2 tablespoons. Saute onions lightly and in another saucepan simmer potatoes until nearly done. Add with all other ingredients, except cream, to bacon and onions, along with whole clams which have been steamed open and their juice strained through a napkin. Simmer 3 or 4 minutes, add cream and serve over crackers in soup plates. If too thick add more milk.

NEW ENGLAND FISH CHOWDER

¼ pound cubed bacon
   or salt pork
1 medium onion sliced
2 pounds haddock
2 cups cubed potatoes

3 cups milk
2 tablespoons butter
salt
freshly ground pepper
crackers

Lightly brown bacon, add onions and saute until soft, add fish and water to cover and cook until firmly done. Meanwhile, simmer potatoes in another pot, add to other mixture with other ingredients and serve over crackers.

CREOLE GUMBO

To the following recipe add about 2 pounds raw cleaned shrimp to simmer about 10 minutes, or 2 dozen large oysters and their liquor to simmer 3 or 4 minutes, or a dozen or so blue crabs, cleaned and halved to simmer 15 mniutes. Instead of the crabs, a pound of crab meat may be used. Shrimps, oysters and crabs may be used in combination in a gumbo and often a 2½ pound disjointed chicken is added to the pot, especially in combination with oysters.

¼ cup drippings
½ pound ham, cubed
1 large garlic, minced
4 scallions and tops, chopped
1 stalk celery and
   leaves, chopped
1 box frozen okra
1 bell pepper, sliced

2 quarts water, about
1 bay leaf
1 pinch thyme
2 teaspoons salt
Tabasco to taste
1 tablespoon chopped parsley
2 tablespoons filé powder

Lightly brown ham in drippings, add white part of scallions and garlic to saute a minute or two, then add all other ingredients, except seafood and filé powder. Let it simmer until vegetables begin to get tender then add sea food and when done shut off heat and stir in filé powder. Cooking latter will cause it to become stringy. Serve gumbo in bowls over big mounds of rice.

OYSTER STEW

People from all over the world come to New York's Grand Central Station and sit at the counter to eat oyster stew the way it has been made there for a little more than a half century.

2 pats butter
½ cup oyster liquor and
    clam broth mixed
¼ teaspoon paprika
¼ teaspoon celery salt

1¼ cups milk
½ teaspoon or more
    Worcestershire
8 large Blue Points
dash paprika

Place 1 pat of butter in soup bowl, other in saucepan over low heat. To butter in saucepan add broth, ¼ teaspoon paprika, celery salt, Worcestershire, and oysters and when oysters begin to curl add milk and bring to boil. Pour into soup bowl with pat of butter and add dash of paprika. Serve with oyster crackers.

LOBSTER BISQUE

1 2½-pound lobster
6 cups water, or less
1 teaspoon chopped parsley
1 tablespoon chopped celery
1 pinch thyme
1 bay leaf
1 tablespoon onion

pinch cayenne
1 teaspoon salt
½ cup white wine
4 tablespoons butter
4 tablespoons flour
1 cup heavy cream
2 tablespoons sherry

Split and clean live lobster, cut it crosswise into several pieces, crack claws, cover with water, add all other ingredients, except last 4 and let simmer 15 minutes. Meanwhile, put butter in saucepan, stir in flour and when it barely begins to turn strain liquor from lobster into flour-butter mixture and let it simmer a few minutes. If too thick add a little milk. Add cream and sherry, bring to boil and pour into bowls containing pieces of lobster.

COURT BOUILLON

This broth, the result of poaching fish to be served as boiled fish, may be served as a soup or used in the preparation of various fish sauces. Fish best suited to this cooking are cod, haddock, channel bass and like salt water fish and salmon, most especially, among fresh water fish. Quantities of ingredients depend upon size of the fish, which may be simmered whole or in serving-sized pieces.

3 tablespoons butter	3 sprigs parsley, chopped
1 medium onion, chopped	pinch of thyme
1 medium carrot, sliced	½ cup white wine
1 stalk celery and leaves, chopped	water
1 bay leaf	salt and pepper

Saute onions in butter until soft, add water and all other ingredients, cover and simmer 20 minutes. Add fish and simmer until done.

CREOLE COURT BOUILLON

Along the Gulf Coast and on into Louisiana, Court Bouillon is a main dish. It could be listed with stews, which is what it is—contrary to oyster stew, for instance, which is a soup. A large channel bass—colloquially red fish—generally is used, cut in thick slices through the backbone, but any large fish will do, as will shrimp.

¼ cup lard or oil	1 bay leaf
5 tablespoons flour	salt and Tabasco
4 scallions and tops, chopped	water
2 cloves garlic, minced	2 pounds fish

Cook flour to a deep brown in lard or oil, add scallions and garlic to saute a minute, then add all other ingredients, except fish. Let simmer 5 minutes, add fish and cook until done with enough water to cover. This invariably is served with white boiled rice.

LOON BAY LODGE STEEPED TROUT

This dish produce a court bouillon or fish stock of sorts to be used in sauces or otherwise, but more importantly it produces a fish dish fit for strong men or invalid babies, as prepared at George Welock's Loon Bay Lodge on the St. Croix in New Brunswick.

Internationally famous for his cuisine, Mr. Welock's preferences in fish are fried trout and his way of boiling trout. An irrevocable rule is that they be cooked almost as soon as caught in a nearby stream.

Remove the insides of the trout and drop them into a pail of cold water with plenty of salt, bring them to a simmer over a high fire and let them steep for a couple of minutes. Serve them with butter and pepper, and a little lemon juice if you like it, along with boiled potatoes.

The Loon Bay Lodge recipe for fried trout will be found in detail a little farther along in this chapter in the section devoted to Fried, Broiled and Sauteed fish.

SICILIAN FISH SOUP

¼ cup olive oil	1 tablespoon parsley, chopped
2 cloves garlic crushed	pinch Italian red pepper
3 cups water, about	1 tablespoon fennel tops, chopped
½ teaspoon oregano	2 pounds heavy fish such as
salt to taste	cod, channel bass, etc.

Saute garlic in oil a minute. Add all other ingredients and simmer until done. Serves 4 or 5.

STEWS

Oyster stew made with milk, bouillabaisse and Creole court bouillon will be found in preceding pages on Chowder, Bisque and Gumbo.

SHRIMP CREOLE

2 pounds shrimp	2 green peppers, sliced
¼ cup olive oil	1 bay leaf
4 tablespoons flour	1 tablespoon chopped parsley
6 scallions and tops, chopped	Tabasco to taste
1 clove chopped garlic	salt to taste
1 cup canned tomatoes	pinch of thyme
1 stalk celery and leaves, chopped	2 cups water

Brown flour in olive oil, add scallions and garlic and saute a minute. Add all other ingredients, except shrimp, and let simmer 15 minutes. Add peeled, de-veined raw shrimp and cook until done, 10 to 15 minutes. Serves 4 or 5 with white rice, a salad and hot rolls or biscuits.

BOUILLABAISSE

Inasmuch as this is eaten from a soup bowl with the sea food usually on the side, it is a meal in itself and probably the world's most renowned fish dish the way it is prepared in Marseilles, France.

⅓ cup olive oil
3 leeks, chopped (white part only)
3 cloves garlic, minced
1 small carrot, grated
3 tomatoes chopped
1 bay leaf
1 tablespoon chopped parsley
2 tablespoons chopped fennel tops

⅛ teaspoon thyme
2 teaspoons salt or more
2 2-pound lobsters, cut up
2 pounds shrimp
2 pounds cod or haddock
2 pounds mackerel
2 pounds red snapper
24 mussels
sliced French bread
scant teaspoon saffron

Saute leeks, onion, garlic and carrot lightly in olive oil. Add fish, cut into slices about an inch thick, lobster cut into pieces through shell, raw shrimp peeled and de-veined, and all other ingredients, except mussels and bread. Add water to almost cover. In separate pot, steam mussels, which have been washed and scraped, and when opened add them to the cooking fish for the last few minutes, along with mussel broth, strained through a napkin. Cook all until done, but not over-cooked, about 15 minutes. Place sliced French bread in soup bowls and pour soup in. Serve fish on side. This will serve a dozen or more.

OTHER SEAFOOD CREOLE

Follow foregoing recipe, using 2 pounds of red snapper, channel bass or other fish, instead of shrimp, or 2 dozen oysters or live crabs. Live crabs, cleaned, the body sections halved and the claws included, makes a better dish of this kind—stew—than does picked crabmeat.

BROWN SHRIMP OR CRAB STEW

Follow recipe for Creole Court Bouillon.

BROWN OYSTER STEW

Same as above, using 2 or 3 dozen oysters and their liquor.

OYSTER PIE

Same as above for filling, placed in deep baking dish lined with and the whole covered with pie crust.

SEAFOOD CURRY

In India and adjacent precincts, curry is made with anything at hand—meats, sea food, or vegetables. In the south it is hot with spices and pepper and in the north more bland. For a basic recipe, see chapter on venison for venison curry.

FISH AND POTATO STEW

Heavy fish, such as cod, channel bass, catfish, red snapper, striped bass should be used in this stew, which is best made in a big iron pot at the beach or on the banks of lake or stream.

½ pound bacon	3 tablespoons chopped parsley
5 pounds fish	salt
3 pounds potatoes, sliced	freshly ground black pepper
1 pound onions, sliced	water

Fry bacon until crisp and set aside. Place in kettle with drippings from bacon, alternate layers of potatoes, onions, a sprinkling of parsley, and cut up pieces of fish. Cover with water. Cover pot and let simmer slowly until done. A dozen or more servings topped with crumbled bacon.

CATFISH STEW AND HUSHPUPPIES

A pot in which to fry or stew catfish is part of the equipment for every catfishing expedition, as is a skillet in which to cook hushpuppies, a recipe for which will be found in the chapter on breads. To make catfish stew, follow recipe for Creole Court Bouillon, but brown ½ inch cubes of bacon or salt pork to obtain drippings in which to brown flour and cook the meat right in with the stew after fat has been rendered. Quantities of ingredients usually is several times larger than the one for the shrimp stew. Simply multiply everything by the quantity of fish to be cooked.

CALAMARI LUCIANO

This squid stew is served over rice or spaghetti at Rapello Restaurant in New York, the recipe supplied by Chef Attilio Poli.

scant ¼ cup olive oil	1½ cups canned
3 pounds squid	plum tomatoes
2 tablespoons olive oil	1 bay leaf
in bud garlic, chopped	¼ teaspoon oregano
1 cup white wine	salt and pepper

Cut squid crosswise into ¼-inch pieces and saute 15 minutes in scant ¼ cup olive oil. Saute garlic in 2 tablespoons olive oil until soft and beginning to turn brown and add to liquid. Add white wine, bay leaf and oregano and simmer 5 minutes. Add tomatoes and simmer 15 minutes longer. Serves 4 or more with green salad and hot Italian bread.

SHRIMP, OKRA AND TOMATOES

3 tablespoons butter	pinch of thyme
1 chopped small onion	1 small bay leaf
1 package frozen okra	salt and pepper
½ cup canned tomatoes	1 pound of shrimp

Saute onion in butter until soft, add tomatoes and seasonings and simmer 5 minutes, add okra, sliced crosswise in ½ inch pieces, and medium sized cleaned raw shrimp. Simmer until done, 10 to 15 minutes. Serves 3 or 4 with white ice. Lump crabmeat stirred in gently may be used instead of shrimp.

SEAFOOD NEWBURG

This may be prepared with boiled lobster, the flesh cut into pieces, shrimp or crabmeat or mixture of the three and bay scallops also sometimes are added.

2 boiled lobsters	4 beaten egg yolks
5 tablespoons butter	3 tablespoons sherry
1½ cups heavy cream	dash paprika
5 raw egg yolks	salt and white pepper

Cut meat from 2 lobsters of about 1¾ pounds into ¾ inch pieces and saute lightly in butter. Add to cream and beaten egg yolks in top of double boiler and cook until thick stirring constantly. Season and add sherry. Serve over toast points to 4 with parsleyed potatoes and green peas and a mild salad.

FROM THE OVEN

BAKED FISH CREOLE

Use large, heavy fish steaks or filets in portion size pieces. Grease bottom of pan with oil, put in the fish and on each piece place a thin slice of lemon. Pour around the fish hot Creole sauce such as is used for shrimp Creole, which see under Stews in this chapter. Bake in 375 degree oven until done, time depending upon thickness of fish. Serve with rice, preferably, or spaghetti or mashed potatoes and usual trimmings.

BAKED FISH WITH LEMON AND BUTTER

Grease bottom of baking pan with enough oil so it will be runny. Place in 425 degree oven until it is hot. Add fish. Bake 10 minutes and place a thin slice of lemon on each piece of fish, pour about ⅓ cup of butter over the fish and squeeze on the juice of a half lemon. Return to oven for about 10 more minutes of baking. Baste a time or two with the butter in the pan. Salt and pepper and serve with or without a fish sauce on the side, parsleyed potatoes and a green vegetable.

BAKED FISH SICILIANO

Follow recipe above, adding 1 or 2 cloves of crushed garlic to pan, and sprinkle with oregano and chopped parsley near end of cooking, along with seasoning to taste.

BAKED CLAMS

2 dozen cherrystones	melted butter
1 tablespoon chopped parsley	salt
freshly ground pepper	bread crumbs
oregano	grated Parmesan

Steam clams in large pot until they open. Remove top shells. Place clams on half shell side by side in baking pan. Add a little of the ingredients in order, finishing with a covering of bread crumbs and a sprinkling of the grated cheese. Bake in 400 degree oven 5 or 6 minutes and serve hot to 2 or more as appetizer or as main dish with salad, vegetables and hot garlic bread.

BAKED CLAMS CASINO

2 doz. cherrystones	2 teaspoons chopped parsley
2 tablespoons minced canned pimentos	2 teaspoons chopped chives
	freshly ground pepper
2 tablespoons minced green pepper	salt
	bacon in pieces

Divide ingredients, except bacon, over clams on half shell and place under broiler for a minute. Cover with a piece of bacon the size of each clam and place back under broiler to cook 6 or 7 minutes, the bacon to be turned once. Serve 2 or more as the appetizer or as main dish with salad, vegetable and garlic bread.

BAKED STUFFED CRABS

1 pound lump crabmeat	4 slices white bread
¼ stick butter	salt
2 tablespoons celery and leaves, chopped	freshly ground pepper
	2 teaspoons chopped parsley
2 tablespoons scallions and leaves chopped	bread crumbs
	paprika

Saute celery and scallions in butter for a minute, add bread soaked in water, partly squeezed out and broken into bits. Add crabmeat, seasoning and parsley and mix gently to avoid breaking up crabmeat lumps. Place mixture in about 4 crab shells, natural or oven wear, sprinkle on bread crumbs, dot with butter, dust with paprika and bake in 400 degree oven until browned. Serves 4 as appetizer or main dish.

LOBSTER THERMIDOR

2 2-pound lobsters	salt
3 tablespoons butter	dash Tabasco
3 tablespoons flour	1 teaspoon chopped parsley
1 tablespoon onion, minced	1 cup light cream
1 teaspoon dry mustard	grated Parmesan
½ cup dry white wine	bread crumbs

Split and clean lobsters and bake 15 minutes in 400 degree oven. Remove meat and cut into ¼ inch pieces. In the meantime, mix butter and flour over low heat, add all other ingredients, except cheese and bread crumbs, and mix thoroughly with lobster meat. Spoon a little sauce in lobster shells, add the lobster mixture, reserving 3 or 4 tablespoons to be spread over top. Cover with bread crumbs, dot with butter, sprinkle on cheese and brown under broiler. Serves 2 or 4 with fried potatoes, a vegetable and sliced tomato salad.

COQUILLES ST. JACQUES

1 pound bay scallops, chopped coarsely (in about 4 pieces)	⅛ teaspoon white pepper
	pinch of thyme
¼ pound mushrooms, choped coarsely	small bay leaf
	5 tablespoons butter
1 cup dry white wine	4 tablespoons flour
1 tablespoon lemon juice	1 tablespoon minced onion
½ teaspoon salt	1 cup heavy cream
1 teaspoon chopped parsley	bread crumbs

Cut up, wash and drain scallops, and simmer 10 minutes in wine and lemon juice, with salt, pepper, thyme, bay leaf and onions, the latter sauted a minute in a little butter. Add mushrooms and simmer another 2 minutes. In another small saucepan, mix butter and flour over low heat without browning, strain into this roux liquid from scallops and add cream and parsley, stirring until smooth and thick. Pour most of this sauce into scallops and mushrooms. Mix thoroughly, spoon the mixture onto scallop shells and spread a little of the reserved sauce over the mixture. Cover with bread crumbs, dot with butter and brown under broiler. This will make 6 servings as an appetizer or a meal with proper accompaniments. To help make it into a main dish add the touch:

OYSTERS ROCKEFELLER

2 dozen oysters	2 teaspoons Pernod (if available)
¼ stick butter	
3 tablespoons minced scallions	2 teaspoons lemon juice
	salt
2 tablespoons minced parsley	dash Tabasco
2 tablespoons chopped celery	¼ cup water, or more
½ cup minced spinach	bread crumbs

Place oysters in baking pan on layer of rock salt to hold them upright. Saute scallions in butter for a minute or two, add all other ingredients and simmer 4 or 5 minutes, stirring. Place some of the mixture on each oyster, sprinkle with bread crumbs, dot with butter and bake about 8 minutes. Serve 2 to 4 as appetizer or main dish.

PARISIENNE

Before putting scallops under broiler, with a pastry bag put a border around the mixture of mashed potatoes mixed with an egg yolk, and brushed with yolk of egg to brown with the scallops.

FRIED, BROILED, SAUTEED

Fried fresh water trout well could be the most favored fish among those who have eaten them, especially in camp or in a fishing lodge after a day on the stream. Along the coast nothing can surpass a fish fry of freshly caught salt water fish on the beach.

Frying fits all fish, but is best with the less fatty ones such as fresh water trout, black bass, flounder, catfish, smelts, weakfish, channel bass and the like. Salmon, large fresh water trout, pompano, shad, mackerel, bluefish, scrod, swordfish and similar fish are best broiled, over or under an open fire. Filets and thin steaks also may be sauteed.

LOON BAY LODGE FRIED TROUT

As previously mentioned under Steeped Trout, George Welock's Loon Bay Lodge on the St. Croix in New Brunswick is widely famous for its fine cuisine and the way they fry your trout is no exception.

Melt a half pound of butter in a heavy skillet over a low flame, then increase the heat and when the butter begins to bubble put in the trout which have been cleaned of innards, lightly salted and peppered and rolled in corn meal. Lower heat and brown slowly, the slower the better, so as to take 25 to 30 minutes to cook. Serve with lemon wedges.

The best eating trout are 7 to 9 inches in length and the trout-fancier simply folds back the top half, lifts out the backbone, cuts off the tail or not, sprinkles on a little lemon juice, folds the top half back into place and eats it like a corn stick. With the trout goes eggs, perhaps, and bacon for breakfast and boiled potatoes and green peas or any vegetable at other times.

Trout also may be fried in bacon drippings or in a mixture of bacon drippings and butter, or rolled in flour instead of corn meal, but Welock's way at Loon Bay Lodge is the best by considerable margin.

OTHER FRIED FISH

Follow foregoing procedure whether small whole fish, filets or steaks. Tarter sauce usually is served on the side and for bread hushpuppies are cooked in the fish-frying fat and served (see hushpuppy recipe in chapter on Breads).

FRIED OYSTERS

Do not use batter on oysters for frying—a common mistake. Salt and pepper the oysters and roll them in cornmeal. Fry quickly in deep hot fat.

BUTTERFLY SHRIMP AND SEAFOOD FRITTERS

Shell raw shrimp, leaving on tails, de-vein, split lengthwise halfway through the shrimp, spread open, roll in flour, dip in batter and fry until brown in deep fat. (See batter in chapter on Breads).

Mix chopped seafood and preferred herbs and spices with batter and pour on greased griddle to cook like hot cakes, or slightly thicken the batter and drop by big spoonfuls into hot fat to brown.

Broiled

Fish to be broiled are usually salted and peppered, coated with a little oil or butter and broiled fast. For such fresh water fish as trout of around 12 inches and salt water fish like pompano broiling is the best way to prepare them, and broiling is suitable for nearly any seafood.

Sauteed

Thin filets or steaks of fish, lightly floured or plain, are often sauteed in a little butter or oil and finished with a garnish of chopped parsley or a covering sauce. Crabmeat and other seafood also lend themselves to this method.

At New York's Voisin restaurant they serve:

SOFT SHELL CRABS GLENOBLOISE

1 doz. soft shell crabs	butter
salt and pepper	lemon
flour	2 tablespoons capers

Clean crabs, salt and pepper, dredge in flour and saute in butter until browned on each side. Remove to serving dish, garnish with lemon slices and sprigs of parsley. Add ⅓ stick of butter to pan, heat to light brown, squeeze in a little lemon juice, add capers and pour over crabs. Serves 4 with potato croquettes, buttered asparagus tips, a salad and hot French bread.

CRAB CAKES

1 pound lump crab meat	salt and pepper
½ cup bread crumbs	1 teaspoon celery seed
2 eggs, beaten	1 tablespoon chopped parsley

Mix ingredients carefully to avoid breaking up crabmeat, add a little more bread crumbs if needed, form into cakes 2½ inches by 1 inch thick, flour each side and brown slowly in butter. Serves 2 to 4 with soft shell crab accompaniments.

SHRIMPS SAUTE

1 pound shrimp	1 clove garlic, crushed
salt and pepper	¼ cup white wine
flour	dash of lemon juice
¼ stick butter	2 teaspoons chopped parsley

Clean, salt and pepper and flour raw or boiled shrimp. Saute in butter until brown. Move to warm plate. Put garlic in skillet to saute a minute, add other ingredients, simmer a minute or two and pour over shrimp. Serves 2 to 4 with hash brown potatoes, a salad and hot Italian bread.

SHRIMPS SAUTE PLAIN

Saute shrimp as in foregoing, but serve with tartar sauce instead of the prepared sauce above.

CHAPTER 7

SOURDOUGH LEGEND

Breads, Stuffings, Dumplings, Pan Cakes, Side Dishes

Believe all you read by historians—the most notorious liars among them being some who wrote about the frontier— and you'll get the notion that the Wild West couldn't have been tamed nor the mountains conquered into giving up their precious metal without the help of sourdough bread.

The truth is that sourdough bread is excellent with game and is the kind which would stick to your ribs for arduous chores of early days like stealing cattle, claim-jumping and stringing up sheep-herders. But they had other bread that saw them through and sourdough probably was less common-place than we have been led to believe. What's wrong with corn meal or flour mixed with salt and water and a soupcon of clean white ashes from the fire to make it rise a little?

You could get along very well without any bread at all, in fact, provided you had a gun and a supply of dried beans, without which no frontiersman would be caught on the prairie, in the mountains or perhaps even a dance hall, warming up to the lady known as Lou since she got run out of Cheyenne.

Without all three—sourdough bread, beans and a gun with which to kill game and innocent bystanders—you were in a bit of a jackpot. You most likely faced slow death by starvation instead of a sudden finish like being run over by a herd of bellowing beef, trapped in a blizzard, given a close crewcut by playful Indians or shot up messing around with a stagecoach carrying Wells Fargo goodies.

So many people faced death from so many avenues that you wonder there were any survivors to settle in Dallas, Phoenix, Dawson, Las Vegas, Cripple Creek and Hollywood to dream about the good old days, with or without sourdough. Regardless of everything, it was sourdough—not the Winchester or Colt, the bronco, lariat, pick and shovel—that was man's chief ally on the frontier, and most especially in the mining camps. That's what the historians seem to say, if you care to believe it.

Thus the term Sourdough for every hobo who divided his time between loitering inside saloons and digging holes in the outside landscape. In Americana, a prospector.

Just how the miner ever got clear claim to that name of Sourdough has never been fully explained. It is likely that Marshal Dillon and Chester, along with the Ridin' Kid from Powder River, Chinamen building the railroads, sod-busters, faro-dealers, saloon-keepers, the 7th Cavalry and others who infested those precincts ate as much sourdough as did the miners. At that, none of them was likely to be surfeited with it.

Making sourdough bread is no monumental chore, to be sure, but it requires more time and effort than simply mixing whatever is handy with some drippings from a bison hump and frying it in grizzly fat. Good sourdough bread requires some attention to details. A regard for such niceties is dissipated in the wilds when you've got a squaw-woman as a roommate a thousand miles from nowhere, and she persists in jabbering at you in Flathead or Blackfoot, and would as soon eat a grasshopper as a square meal.

Moreover, there wasn't time to be messing around making a starter for the bread, waiting for it to rise and baking it in an uncertain oven or none at all. If you were the blue and gold of the 7th Cavalry you were too busy chasing Crazy Horse, Sitting Bull or Chitterling Sam; as a ranch hand you were preoccupied with rounding up the cows or being rounded up by Mister Dillon and Chester; and if you were a miner, fixing to uncover the Comstock or some such, your time was devoted to digging nuggets big as sombreros.

What bread—sourdough or otherwise? It will be beans and drippings for dinner tonight as a change from the drippings and beans at breakfast.

Here is the way you make sourdough bread, or the way I make it, among the guests there being always somebody who would prefer a bucket of spaghetti to the wild game and an Italian loaf or French roll instead of sourdough bread, despite my protestations that it is the best and proved it by winning the West.

It approaches other white bread in taste and texture and is easy enough to prepare once a so-called starter has been established. This is the batter containing yeast. You leave some of this batter, rebuild the quantity with flour and water and the yeast continues to grow. It is ready again for the next batch of bread and again only part of it is used, more flour and water are added and it might go on indefinitely, the growing yeast always replenishing itself.

The starting point is making the so-called starter:

1—Place in a 3 or 4-quart bowl or jar, the latter with a top that fits loosely—not one screwed on tightly unless you want to risk blowing up the joint—2 cups of tepid water and 1 envelope of active dry yeast;

2—Stir and let stand 15 minutes;

3—Stir in 2 tablespoons sugar until dissolved;

4—Stir in 2½ cups flour to make a fairly thick batter;

5—Set the bowl or jar in a warm—not hot or cold—place covered lightly with a napkin or jar-lid for 10 or 12 hours;

To make the sourdough bread:

1—Remove 1 cup of the starter into another bowl;

2—Stir into this starter 1 teaspoon baking powder and beat with spoon to assure thorough mixing;

3—Stir in 1 tablespoon cooking oil and again beat to mix;

4—Stir in 1 cup of flour and as you knead the dough for 3 or 4 minutes add more flour up to about ½ cup.

5—Shape into a round, slightly flattened loaf and place in a small greased pan, 4 or 5 inches square or in diameter and 1 or 2 inches deep.

6—Let rise in a warm—not hot or cold—place for 2 hours.

7—Pre-heat oven to 425 degrees and bake the loaf 25 to 35 minutes.

During the rising the loaf should more than double in thickness and bulge out over the edge of the pan, from which it should be removed after baking and propped on edge to cool before cutting.

This recipe is for a comparatively small quantity to serve about 4, but may be increased. The bread will be better if baked in these small loaves as suggested.

To the left-over starter—after you have used one cup of it to make the bread—add about 1 cup each of flour and water and in 10 hours or so it will be ready for another batch, after which replenish the starter again with flour and water.

You will find recipes calling for more shortening than is used here or for no shortening, or for the addition of baking soda, potatoes, salt and what-not. These things are not recommended and the recipe provided here is the one that works best for me. However, experiment and you may hit upon something you like better.

OTHER BREADS

As a preface to the making of corn bread, let it be said that the corn meal produced when corn is ground between stones is infinitely better than machine-ground meal. What is referred to as best is so-called water-ground meal—because the stones generally are turned by waterwheel—and in this meal is preserved the germ of the grain as well as most of the husk.

Stone-ground meal is softer in texture than the white or yellow machined meal, and it has a sweet, nut-like flavor which produces what to many is the best bread in the world.

It can be fancied up or be as simple as:

HOE CAKES

To make 4 big servings, mix 2 cups of stone-ground cornmeal with 1 teaspoon salt and stir in enough boiling water to make a dough that is a little on the thin side, but not runny. Heat a big iron skillet over a medium low fire, grease it lightly with bacon drippings and spread in the dough about ½ inch thick or spoon the dough in and spread it into smaller cakes of the same thickness. Brown slowly on each side. Split open and spread with butter and serve with any game or fish.

FANCY HOE CAKES

1 cup corn meal	1 beaten egg
¾ cup flour	¾ cup milk
½ teaspoon salt	3 tablespoons butter or oil
2 teaspoons baking powder	

Sift dry ingredients together, mix beaten egg and milk and mix all together with butter or oil. Spread about ½ inch thick in skillet heated over medium low fire and lightly greased with bacon drippings or make into smaller cakes. Brown on each side and when done split and apply butter. Serves 4.

CORN BREAD

Incidentally, these various breads are not supposed to be crumbly, flossy productions, but delicate enough beneath the veneer of robustness.

Use the recipe for Fancy Hoe Cake, but put the dough in a greased baking pan to the thickness of a big inch and bake in a 375 degree oven for 40 minutes.

CORN MUFFINS

Follow foregoing, but add 2 teaspoons of sugar to dough and bake in muffin tin.

CORN STICKS

Follow recipe for Fancy Hoe Cake, but use ½ teaspoon baking soda instead of the baking powder, and buttermilk, instead of sweet milk. Bake in greased corn stick pan.

TALLAHASSEE HUSH PUPPIES

1 cup cornmeal
1 teaspoon baking powder
½ teaspoon salt
1 beaten egg
¼ cup water, or more
1 medium onion minced

Sift the dry ingredients together, and mix with the others. Form into oblong cakes about 2 inches in length, 1 inch wide and ½ inch thick and deep fry in fat in which fish were fried if accompanying fried fish. Serves 3 or 4.

CAMP BISCUITS

2 cups flour
2 teaspoons baking powder
½ teaspoon salt
2 tablespoons shortening
¾ cup milk or water

Sift and mix dry ingredients and cut in the shortening. Add milk or water. Mix thoroughly and knead briefly until smoothly mixed and roll out dough to about ¾ inch thickness on floured board. Cut into fairly large biscuits and bake at 425 degrees 15 minutes or until brown. Serves about 4.

CAMP SOUR MILK BISCUITS

2 cups flour   ¾ teaspoon baking soda
½ teaspoon salt   ¾ cup buttermilk
3 tablespoons shortening   or sour milk

Sift flour and salt, cut in shortening, stir soda into milk and mix all thoroughly. Roll out to about ¾ inch in thickness and cut into fairly large biscuits. Bake at 425 degrees for 15 minutes or until brown.

YORKSHIRE PUDDING

Despite its high-sounding name, Yorkshire Pudding is easy to prepare and goes as well with a roast of venison and such, as it does with roast beef. It should be prepared in advance, which see in the following directions.

1 cup flour   1 cup milk
½ teaspoon salt   2 eggs

Sift salt and flour together, add milk and stir and beat until smooth. Add eggs 1 at a time and beat thoroughly with rotary beater, 2 or 3 minutes after addition of each egg. Cover mixture and set in the refrigerator for about 2 hours. Heat a pan very hot containing 3 tablespoons drippings and pour batter into it. Place in 450 degree oven for 15 minutes, then reduce heat to 350 and cook another 15 minutes. Slice and serve on side. Serves 4.

POPOVERS

The batter is identical in quantities with that prepared for Yorkshire Pudding. Grease and pre-heat popover pan and, without putting batter in the refrigerator, only half fill popover containers. They will rise well beyond the surface of the pan. This recipe makes 8 popovers.

For a variation, put about a tablespoon of batter into the hot popover compartments, sprinkle in some crumbled cheddar cheese, then pour over enough batter to half fill compartments.

DUMPLINGS

1 cup flour	pinch white pepper
½ teaspoon salt	1 tablespoon unmelted butter
2 teaspoons baking powder	½ cup milk

Sift dry ingredients together and rub or cut in butter. Add milk and mix with least amount of stirring. Drop a rounded tablespoon of the dough into stew so it rests on meat and is only partly submerged, with stew simmering, not rapidly boiling. Cover and without uncovering again cook dumplings 15 minutes. Serves 2 to 4.

HERB DUMPLINGS

Add ¼ teaspoon each of oregano, chopped chives and parsley, a pinch of powdered sage and a little more pepper to above mixture.

CORNMEAL DUMPLINGS

Use half flour and half waterground cornmeal and follow foregoing recipes.

POTATO DUMPLINGS

The following recipe for potato dumplings is from Luchow's old and famous New York restaurant:

2 pounds (6) raw potatoes	1 teaspoon minced parsley
10 slices bread	2 eggs, well beaten
1 teaspoon salt	¼ cup flour
¼ teaspoon pepper	1½ quarts boiling
1 onion, grated	salted water

Wash, peel and grate potatoes. Soak bread in a little cold water; squeeze out as much water as possible. Mix bread, salt, pepper, onions and parsley. Add potatoes and eggs, mix well. Form into balls, roll lightly in flour, drop into boiling salted water (1 teaspoon salt to each quart water). Cover pot tightly; boil 15 minutes. Serves 4 or more.

CORN DODGERS

These heavy dumplings usually are prepared with mustard, turnip or collard greens, which are cooked with salt pork, bacon or ham hock in ample water to make enough pot likker to go around, being served with the vegetables and meat and dumplings in soup plates.

1 cup waterground meal	2 tablespoons drippings
½ teaspoon salt	

Mix all ingredients into a sticky dough and spoon rounded tablespoon of the dough into the pot to rest partly submerged on the vegetables. Simmer covered 15 minutes. Serves 2 to 4.

HOT CAKES

REGULAR HOT CAKES

1 cup flour	¾ cup milk
1 teaspoon baking powder	1 beaten egg
½ teaspoon salt	2 tablespoons melted butter
1 teaspoon sugar	

Sift dry ingredients together, add the egg and butter and milk and beat thoroughly to remove lumps and lighten, adding a little more milk, if necessary. Brown on both sides in greased skillet or on greased griddle over medium low flame, turning once. Serves 2 or 3.

BUTTERMILK HOT CAKES

Charlie Collins, director of the Milwaukee Sports and Travel Show, is known far beyond the boundaries of Wisconsin for what he calls Cedar Grove Buttermilk Pancakes:

1 cup flour	1 teaspoon baking soda
1 teaspoon sugar	1¼ cups buttermilk
pinch of salt	1 beaten egg

Sift dry ingredients together and mix with egg and buttermilk without any butter or other shortening. Brown as in foregoing recipe.

BUCKWHEAT CAKES

¾ cup buckwheat	¾ cup milk
¼ cup white flour	1 tablespoon molasses
1 teaspoon baking powder	1 beaten egg
¼ teaspoon salt	2 tablespoons melted butter

Proceed as in above recipes.

WILD RICE HOT CAKES

Add ¾ cup cooked wild rice and a little more salt to foregoing recipes.

CORN MEAL AND APPLE HOT CAKES

In recipes for Regular Hot Cakes and Buttermilk Hot Cakes use ½ flour and ½ water-ground cornmeal, ½ cup finely chopped apples and pinch of nutmeg.

POTATO PANCAKES

2 pounds potatoes	1 teaspoon salt
2 tablespoons flour	¼ teaspoon pepper
1 small onion, grated	⅛ teaspoon nutmeg
2 eggs lightly beaten	bacon drippings

Grate raw potatoes, discard liquid, mix grated potato and all other ingredients. Spoon onto hot griddle or into hot skillet greased lightly with bacon drippings and cook until done on each side.

FRITTERS

The basic preparation for fritters may be called a thin dough or a thick batter, thicker than the batter for hot cakes, as an example, in that this batter for fritters is supposed to cover rather than be a part of the food to be deep fried. Vegetables, fruits, meats, sea food all may be dipped in batter and then fried either in deep fat or at least in enough fat to nearly cover—and it should be hot. A recipe for this batter:

1 cup flour	3 beaten eggs
1 teaspoon baking powder	scant ¼ cup milk
¼ teaspoon salt	pinch of pepper

Sweet fritters made with fruit and the like should be quickly drained of grease on paper napkins and served hot with a sprinkling of powdered sugar. Other fritters are served generally as an accompaniment to other dishes.

READY MIXES

There is some resistance on the part of cooks to use any of the innumerable packaged mixes obtainable in stores for the various hot breads covered in the foregoing on the grounds that there is nothing like good old home-made stuff.

There is much to be said for that viewpoint, but something to be said against it, too. Packaged and frozen mixes are for the most part good and save a lot of time.

Moreover, there is nothing new about this. Frontiersmen invented it.

Compelled to leave the old mud-chinked, log manse for a trip of a few days or weeks, cattleman, sheep-herder, woodsman or who not often mixed up available dry ingredients to last the trip and made his biscuits or hoe cake as needed. He might use bear grease, venison or bison suet for shortening, but most often salt pork drippings, and water to wet it down. Water because there wasn't any milk and, moreover, milk tends to dry out faster than water in bread.

In the absence of baking powder, he also might use wood ashes to make his bread rise a little—the white part of the ashes from hardwood alone being recommended.

Ashes, in fact, are very useful. When hot you may roast a potato or ear of corn and the like in the ashes, and they may be used with proper additives for tanning a hide. It is said that the Choctaws boiled dried corn in a solution of ashes and water to make whole hominy among the 30 odd uses they found for corn without a pot to cook in or a window to throw it out of.

STUFFINGS

Few birds in all history ever achieved honors surpassing what happened to the turkey and accompanying stuffing some 25 years ago through the accidental collaboration of the late Morton Thompson, Hollywood newspaper columnist, Chryson's, Ltd., Burbank, California, purveyors of elite Christmas cards, and Larry MacPhail, then running the Brooklyn Dodgers baseball club.

Thompson wrote one of his daily essays on how to cook a turkey; Chryson's reprinted it as a 10-page limited edition Christmas card, and MacPhail was so smitten that he sent to a limited circle of friends and sports writers copies of the limited edition in a bright red envelope as his Christmas card in 1941.

Morton Thompson has since died, but Cryson's, Ltd., continues successful production of most lavish Christmas cards. MacPhail, having left the Dodgers to go into World War II as a colonel—after having tried to kidnap the Kaiser as a captain in World War I—finished his sometimes boisterous baseball operations as co-owner of the New York Yankees and now is a breeder of race horses and beef cattle in Maryland.

The tribute to the turkey, combining the efforts of such diverse personalities dealt with the tame turkey, but the latter is, of course, a direct descendant of the so-called Monarch of American Game Birds, which helped our founding Pilgrim fathers through many a hard winter, with native cranberry sauce on the side. Anyhow, we are not so much concerned here with the turkey as with the stuffing fabricated by Morton Thompson. It is equally suitable to the wild and the domesticated Monarch, if you are prepared to put on your overalls and go to work.

The stuffing is so laborious in preparation, unique in ingredients and so ideally suited to the cook who seeks ornate elaboration that we herewith help perpetuate the recipe.

Salt and pepper the bird inside and out and go ahead and make the stuffing.

Dice 1 apple, 1 orange in a bowl and add to this bowl a large can of crushed pineapple, the grated rind of ½ lemon, 1 can of drained water chestnuts, 3 tablespoons of chopped preserved ginger.

In another bowl put 2 teaspoons Coleman's mustard, 2 teaspoons caraway seed, 3 teaspoons celery seed, 2 teaspoons poppy seed, 2½ teaspoons oregano, 1 well-crushed large bay leaf, 1 teaspoon black pepper, ½ teaspoon mace, 4 tablespoons well-chopped parsley, 4 or 5 finely minced cloves garlic, 4 cloves, minus the heads and well-chopped, ½ teaspoon tumeric, 4 large well-chopped onions, 6 well-chopped stalks celery, ½ teaspoon marjoram, ½ teaspoon savoury (summer savoury if you can get it), and 1 tablespoon poultry seasoning. Some like sage, some like thyme. Nobody, apparently, objects to poultry seasoning, which, ironically, contains both. Salt to taste.

In another bowl dump 3 packages bread crumbs, bought at a bakery. Add to this ¾ pound ground veal, ¼ pound ground fresh pork and ¼ pound butter and all the fat (first rendered) you have been able to find and pry loose from the turkey. Mix in each bowl the contents of each bowl. When each bowl is well-mixed, mix the three of them together. And mix it well. Mix it·with your hands. Mix it until your forearms and wrists ache. Then mix it some more. Now toss it enough so that it isn't any longer a doughy mass.

Then you stuff the bird loosely, truss it and roast it in a way reminscent of the type of outdoor cookery wherein you coat fish or fowl with clay, then roast it.

First you put on to cook a basting liquid composed of the chopped gizzard, heart and neck, a bay leaf, 1 teaspoon paprika, ½ teaspoon coriander, a clove of garlic and 4 cups of water. Proceed with roasting the turkey which has been duly filled with that stuffing.

Turn on the oven full blast to get as hot as possible while you make a paste consisting of the yolks of 2 eggs, a teaspoon dry mustard, a clove of garlic minced, a tablespoon onion juice, a half teaspoon salt, 2 pinches cayenne pepper, 1 teaspoon lemon juice, and enough flour to make a stiff paste.

Put the turkey on a rack in the roasting pan and put it in the hottest possible oven to brown quickly all over. Remove the turkey, turn the oven down to 325 and paint the hot turkey all over with a brush with a coating of the paste. Put it back into the oven to let the paste dry and go through this process of applying paste until it is all used up.

Now you add to the giblet broth 1 cup cider and 2 hookers dark rum and turn off the heat, but keep the stock where it will remain warm. With this, baste the bird every 15 minutes. After the bird has cooked an hour or so, turn it over to be back in the air, then turn it over again, back down, for the last 15 minutes of cooking, which should be 3-½ hours for a wild turkey of around 15 pounds.

There is one more step to all this. When you remove the turkey from the oven ready for the table it will be dead black. But you take a pair of tweezers and pry loose the parched coating of paste you put on it and exposed will be a juicy browned bird.

Like I say, you put on your overalls and go to work.

The following stuffings may be made in more or less quantity for any game birds. For a small turkey decrease the amounts and for a large one make more stuffing, and use your judgment similarly for preparing these stuffings for wild geese and ducks.

APPLE AND PRUNE GOOSE STUFFING

¼ ·stick butter	15 dried prunes
¼ cup chopped celery and leaves	2 teaspoons chopped fresh basil
5 apples	pinch of black pepper

Melt butter over low heat, add all ingredients and mix thoroughly until well heated, the apples having been peeled, cored and quartered and the prunes seeded and halved. Quantity is for average sized wild goose. For other fowl use judgment as to quantity.

ONION GOOSE STUFFING

¼ stick butter	¼ teaspoon sage
4 medium onions sliced	⅛ teaspoon pepper
5 cups crumbled stale bread	pinch salt
pinch of thyme	giblet or canned stock

Saute onions in butter and add all other ingredients, the quantity of stock enough to dampen.

SAUERKRAUT GOOSE STUFFING

¼ stick butter	½ cup giblet or canned stock
¼ cup chopped onion	1 teaspoon caraway seed
3 pounds sauerkraut	black pepper
2 apples	salt

Saute onions in butter. Run water over sauerkraut in sieve, squeeze out, add to onions and butter along with apples which have been peeled, cored and cut into eighths, and all other ingredients. Let simmer until hot, drain and stuff bird.

FISH STUFFING

Bread Stuffing, Corn Bread Stuffing, Oyster Stuffing or Wild Rice Stuffing all may be used to stuff a large fish for baking. Crab meat may be used in place of oysters. A half teaspoon or more of grated lemon rind also may be added.

BREAD STUFFING

1 stick butter
½ cup chopped onion
½ cup chopped celery
  and leaves
2 tablespoons chopped parsley
2 teaspoons salt
¼ teaspoon freshly
  ground pepper
8 cups crumbled stale bread,
  about
½ cup giblet or canned stock
¼ teaspoon thyme
1½ teaspoons dried sage

Saute onions and celery in butter lightly, add all other ingredients and mix thoroughly while heating without browning. Use a little more or a little less stock, but avoid a soggy dressing and do not pack into the bird tightly.

CORN BREAD STUFFING

Follow foregoing, but make a pan of corn bread according to corn bread recipes and use this instead of white bread.

OYSTER STUFFING

Add a dozen or more large oysters coarsely chopped and their liquor to either of above stuffings.

CHESTNUT STUFFING

Cut a slit in the hull of each of a pound of chestnuts (or a little more), roast, peel, slice and add them to either the Bread Stuffing or the Corn Meal Stuffing or combine with the oysters.

WILD RICE STUFFING

Instead of using bread or corn bread, thoroughly wash and drain 2½ cups wild rice, cover generously with stock and let simmer. After 20 minutes add ingredients in Bread Stuffing and continue to simmer until most of the liquid has been absorbed and rice is firmly done, but not soft, about 10 minutes.

SIDE DISHES

The American Indian is established among the most defamed and abused peoples on earth, and he seldom gets slightest recognition for his contributions to a better way of life for his unappreciative pale-faced foe.

The movies, TV and printed folklore have done the Red Man sad injustice, depicting him always killing handsome kindly members of the U. S. Cavalry (who die whispering home-spun humor), sacking a defenseless village (where the Red Man's wickiup stood until he was chased), burning a wagon train (which has stampeded the winter's supply of bison), or raising unprovoked hell in general.

His motivations are inevitably the same, the way he is presented to us who know him only from a distance and couldn't care less. His violence is fueled by whiskey fit only for drowning tarantulas; his indolence personified by a blanketed, drowsy brave on haunches braced against a frontier building, with a feather in his hat. Then there is the rich Indian, the one who has struck oil and moved into a Tulsa mansion with a Cadillac on the side. Thinking he has stumbled upon a new kind of sweet water spring in the bathroom, he is drinking from the toilet bowl.

The Red Man is never shown gathering wild rice.

But he not only does gather this grain each fall mainly in Wisconsin and Minnesota, he has been doing it so long that there is a tribe of Indians known as Menominee, as well as a Wisconsin city, a Michigan city and a river by that name, Spelled out it is wild rice, rhyming loosely with hominy, converted from corn by the Choctaws—another point in favor of the red man.

Wild rice now has a fairly wide range east of the Mississippi and on up into Canada, and it has been transplanted to Europe and the Orient. On some tables it is as important to a game dinner as the meat itself, almost.

You may prepare it as you would white rice, but it takes longer to cook. Some wild rice fanciers advocate soaking it in water 10 to 12 hours, which is a matter of choice. In any case, run warm water over it through a sieve and wash it thoroughly.

WILD RICE AND MUSHROOMS

2 cups wild rice	2 cups sliced mushrooms
8 cups canned broth	salt and pepper
2 tablespoons minced onion	⅓ stick butter

Simmer the wild rice in canned chicken or beef broth or broth made with game trimmings or giblets, until the broth has been absorbed and the rice is tender, adding more broth if necessary. The cooking time will be about 45 minutes.

After about 25 minutes of the cooking, stir in the onions and mushrooms which have been lightly sauteed in the butter, and the salt and pepper. If the stock contains salt be careful of over-salting the rice. This quantity will serve 6 or 8, and it may be further seasoned with chopped parsley, celery leaves, thyme or to suit your preference.

WHITE RICE

Prepare it according. to package instructions or by foregoing recipe, observing instructions on amount of liquid and cooking time.

HOMINY

Whole canned hominy need be only heated in butter with salt and pepper or with cut up sauteed bacon or ham to accompany fish or game or as a breakfast dish may be scrambled with eggs.

HOMINY GRITS

Prepare it according to package instructions as a side dish with butter. Left-over grits may be sliced into squares an inch thick, dipped in egg and flour and pan fried in butter or drippings.

WHITE POTATOES

Small, red-skinned new potatoes scraped, simmered until done, buttered and sprinkled with parsley are to some people the finest eating potatoes in the world, but they will get an argument expressing that viewpoint in company devoted to a big, baked, buttered Idaho. Ordinary old potatoes have their uses, too, in stew, chowders and the like.

The small new potatoes cooked with a little bacon or ham and green beans make a side dish that leaves little room for anything else, except perhaps a salad, and that potato and green bean dish is notoriously fine if carefully prepared so that neither the potatoes nor the beans are over-cooked. Chopped scallion tops added near the end of cooking may be to your liking. A few drops of hot pepper vinegar, too, perhaps.

After plain boiling, the small new potatoes also may be sauteed whole in butter or drippings until lightly browned and served just that way or with touches of chopped pimiento.

The baked Idaho is a national favorite, requiring about 40 minutes in a hot oven, depending upon size. Butter, salt and pepper may be replaced by sour cream, chopped chives, salt and pepper, in which case, after scooping out the potato and mixing it with the other ingredients, put the refilled potato back into the oven to heat for a few minutes. Before baking, wash the Idaho and scrub it, dry it and grease it with cooking oil for appearance, and to eat skin and all. Chop left-over baked potatoes and hash-brown in butter or drippings.

The excellence of baked potatoes in some Irish restaurants comes of their way of preparing medium-sized, round potatoes. They are washed thoroughly, boiled 15 minutes or so in heavily salted water, then baked until done.

The Idaho makes unsurpassed fried potatoes when cut into strips less than a half inch square and fried without any pre-cooking. For texture and extra crispness roll the strips in cornmeal before putting into the hot fat.

A number of other potato preparations will be found in other chapters.

SWEET POTATOES

Baking and boiling with the skin on are the most popular methods of preparing sweet potatoes, which go with any game. Often they are peeled and cooked along with a roast. Baked or boiled, they may be buttered and lightly seasoned with a little salt and pepper, or mashed with butter and milk or orange juice. They also may be sliced and fried in drippings and served with bacon.

RED CABBAGE

This is regarded by many as almost a must with roast goose.

1 medium head red cabbage	⅛ teaspoon black pepper
1 small minced onion	1 teaspoon sugar
2 tablespoons butter	2 tablespoons vinegar
1 teaspoon salt	pinch nutmeg

Discard outer leaves of cabbage, chop rest and simmer with other ingredients until done in water or canned chicken stock to cover.

CHAPTER 8

THE ROMANCE OF IT ALL

Herbs, Spices, Bottled Sauces, Wines

The greatest romance concerning food and the oldest centers around the spice trade with its history of exploration, intrigue, discovery of new far corners, survival and failures of empires, going back 2,000 years before Christ.

By the time the Egyptians got through inventing civilization and passed it on to the Greeks for refinement and they in turn noted its spread around the then world by the Phonecians, spices were next in importance to gold and precious stones in bartering for slaves and similar attractive baubles.

When somebody reproves you for supposedly spoiling a good steak with ketchup, as some one always does, remind the boor that this mixture of tomatoes and vinegar cooked down with pepper, cloves and the rest bears a trace of history that goes back to acquisitive seafarers in craft scarcely bigger than skiffs. This bottled goods savors of the seven seas, a thousand conquests, time beyond accurate record and laden caravans on the weary journey.

Say, too, if your audience is still with you, that when Hippocrates, Socrates, Aristotle, Plato and those other Greeks visited with each other, they did not open a one-arm lunch. Instead they walked in the garden and dreamed up philosophy and Democracy for us, while eating pepper to settle a nervous stomach and chewing wild thyme from Mount Hymettus because it tasted good.

91

For a sack of the right spices a man would risk his life and could buy a whole harem or a horde of politicians, and go a long way toward outfitting an army to pillage wherever the pickings were lushest. Everybody wanted the stuff, and pepper perhaps more so than anything else. This now common and cheap commodity helped to make Genoa and Venice the biggest of trade centers into the 15th century. Then Portugal had a fling at the early day wheeling and dealing, and it began to spread gradually through the centuries around the world. What generated this original boost for the good old peppercorn was sudden discovery by various citizens that it is an invaluable food preservative.

This early trade was by comparison as big as steel or automobiles today—maybe bigger—and while this merchandising of pepper and the other spices no longer is that important it is not an industrial dwarf. In the United States alone some 50,000,000 pounds of pepper is used up each year. Add some more millions of pounds covering the other spices and you get a fair picture of the hold that seeds, berries, leaves, blossoms, bark and roots of plant life have had on man and of the value involved in days of uncertain transportation.

Even now, if you could hi-jack, say, a hundred pounds of Spanish saffron and dispose of it at going retail prices you could bank around $5,000. But pepper is in a slump. The ransom in a siege of Rome by the Goths included 3,000 pounds of pepper (along with some gold and other desirables, to be sure). A pound of peppercorns today retail for about a buck fifty, give or take a lira. Thus 3,000 pounds would come to little more than a fortnight's binge in Rome for an ever-loving couple from the USA.

Then there is the romance of cloves. Every sneak-drinker knows that these dried buds are as good as Sen-Sen and better than parsley for sweetening the breath, which is no brand new discovery. Backtrack through some hundreds of years and you will find that lovers unacquainted with Listerine and Lavoris munched cloves before heaving close up sighs toward a victim of affections. Likewise, in some garlic-eating countries they would part your hair in the middle at the nape of the neck with a guillotine to teach you a lesson for conferring with a high official without first indulging in the clove department.

Going no farther, we can perceive that the spice rack contains not merely bottles and packets filled with inconsequentials. That's the whole gamut of history, neatly labelled and awaiting destiny in a fricassee at home, a beef-stew at the corner saloon or in a potentate's banquet hall.

Of the hundreds of herbs, spices and seasonings available from fields, forests and jungles all over the world—and even from the ocean which supplies seaweed used in some exotic sauces—you can get by very well with a dozen and an occasional purchase for some special preparation. In time they lose their strength, and should be bought as needed.

The herbs and spices—generally grouped as aromatics—most essential in cooking are bay leaves, basil, thyme, oregano, paprika, sage, powdered mustard, rosemary and savory.

Occasionally you will need curry powder, saffron and dill—the latter preferably fresh—but these can be bought when the occasion demands. The same applies pretty much to tarragon, marjoram, nutmeg, cloves, cinnamon and the like.

Salt, of course, is indispensible, as is pepper, both classed as seasonings, the latter including whole peppercorns to be ground as needed, ground white pepper and a red hot pepper such as cayenne or Tabasco.

Onions and garlic lead the seasoning vegetables, followed closely by parsley—used for taste and as a garnish—scallions, eschallots, celery and green bell peppers.

Among the essentials in acids for the tart touch are vinegar and lemon juice. Red or white wine vinegar is best, but there is a wide choice through malt, cider and distilled vinegars.

Lined up end to end, the bottled sauces would stretch into the stratosphere. Worcestershire—and by that is meant Lea and Perrins—probably heads the list in the kitchen followed by ketchup, chili sauce, prepared mustard, prepared horseradish, A-1 sauce, Durkee's and Escoffier Diable.

A word as to mustard, one of the best and yet least used is the bottled Creole mustard from New Orleans. Another is the French Dijon.

An almost must on the spice shelf which is too little used is monosodium glutemate, obtainable under the trade name Accent. This is a vegetable derivative, which brings out the flavor of any soup or sauce and is widely used in restaurant kitchens. It adds no distinctive taste, but rather strengthens stock or sauce and is highly recommended in recipes for brown and white sauce.

In the use of all the foregoing, extreme care must be taken not to overdo it. Too much is worse than none at all. This applies to using too much of any one item or combining too many. The basic taste of food should not be destroyed by extraneous flavor. You don't cook game or fish to make herbs and the like taste better, but vice versa, except in rare instances where pepper, for example, can be nearly overpowering in a dish such as chili con carne.

Wines are not as commonly used in cookery in this country as they are in European households, but there has been a steady growth and many kitchens include among the flavorings at least a bottle of sherry, which is the most important of the wine flavorings.

American wines will work as well as any, and after sherry come a dry red wine and a dry white wine. You can make do with that, but it is better to include a Marsala type, or a Port, so often specified in game cookery.

Brandy will be needed occasionally and can be obtained in a small-sized bottle, if your liquor closet is without it and that about completes the flavoring needs, except for casual mention of one item for one dish. An old-fashioned American apple pie is at its topmost best when the filling of apples is laced with a slug of good American Bourbon.

INDEX

95